CANARIES SOMETIMES SING

CANARIES
SOMETIMES SING?.

A COMEDY IN THREE ACTS

BY

FREDERICK LONSDALE

METHUEN & CO. LTD.
36 ESSEX STREET W.C.
LONDON

First Published in 1930

PRINTED IN GREAT BRITAIN

PRODUCED AT THE GLOBE
THEATRE, LONDON
OCTOBER 21st, 1929

CAST

GEOFFREY LYMES . .	RONALD SQUIRE
ANNE LYMES	MABEL SEALBY
ERNEST MELTON . . .	ATHOLE STEWART
ELMA MELTON . . .	YVONNE ARNAUD

CANARIES SOMETIMES SING

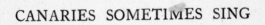

ACT I

Scene: The sitting-room in Geoffrey Lyme's country house.

(Geoffrey *is seated facing a table. On the table is a canary in a cage—he is feeding it.*)

Geoff. You're a naughty little feller—that's what you are! And I have a very good mind not to give you your dinner! Why don't you ever laugh or sing? Eh? Why don't you? Perhaps you hate being in a cage? But we're all of us in a cage of some sort, little feller—and some of us are not alone in it! Good God, Percy, don't tell me the reason you never laugh or sing is because you are alone in it? You fool! Don't you realise how lucky you are—don't you know that I and millions of others would give nearly all we have in the world to change places with you! 'Ssh! In confidence! (*Looks at door, whispers.*) Supposing you had some one in your cage like I have in mine—some one who bored you to death with her stupidities—every time she opened her mouth you nearly screamed—who does nothing that entitles you to divorce her—but who does a thousand things that entitle you to murder her! How would you like your cage filled with the highbrow fellers of the world—who furnished your cage like this one is furnished—look at it—she'll tell you it's artistic! Look at the cloth on the piano—here—(*Rises, pulls it off piano, throws it into cupboard*)—that I won't stand any longer! That's made you think a bit, hasn't it, Percy? You'd turn her out, you say! Getting them into your cage is as easy as getting them out is difficult; that's why only twenty thousand people get divorced a year! Supposing you had some one in there like that? Being a gentleman you would have to bear your mistake in silence—smile when you could strike—and to the world pretend a happiness that does not exist! If this were my case only, Percy, I would not speak, but I am telling you the story of countless thousands of men and women who smile in every other home but their own! Go on, don't be a fool, realise how lucky you are, and sing!

ANNE. (*Heard off.*) Is Mr. Lymes at home, Morton?

MORTON.   In the sitting-room, ma'am.

GEOFF. (*To canary.*) 'Ssh! Here she is, back to my cage for the week-end. Listen to her when she comes in—then if you think I have exaggerated—been unnecessarily cynical—and you still want a mate—well, I'll hate doing it—but I'll buy you one!

ANNE.   (*Off.*)   Geoffrey !

GEOFF.   In here, darling !

> (ANNE *enters ; she is carrying some books,
> which she places on table.*)

> (*Walks to her.*)   Ah, my love, how are you ?

ANNE.   (*Puts up her cheek to be kissed.*)   So tired,
so terribly tired.

GEOFF.   I was afraid you would be, darling !

ANNE.   And so unhappy that little husband isn't
pleased to see his wife !

GEOFF.   What makes you say that ?

ANNE.   Because he didn't come to meet poor
little wife in the car, and let her come all the way
from the station alone in a nasty taxi !

GEOFF.   You didn't let me know what train you
were coming by !

ANNE.   (*Shakes her head.*)   When we were first
married you liked little wife so much you met all
the trains !

GEOFF.   True !   (*Nods his head.*)   True !   Tell
me, you've had a busy week, eh ?

ANNE.   Terrible !   I've never stopped a minute !
And I have such an awful week in front of me !
Do you know, poor little woman has discovered
she is on the committee of three charity
matinées !

GEOFF.   Why be on three ?

ANNE. They insist! Even when I refuse they put poor Anne's name on the committee!

GEOFF. Ghastly for you!

ANNE. Three luncheon-parties in my own house! Four dinner-parties; and last night, tired out, they took me on to night club after night club— poor little wifey didn't get home until nearly four!

GEOFF. Little husband was in bed at ten!

ANNE. Little husband a very lazy man to live in the country as he does; he should come, to London and help his little Anne!

GEOFF. You move in too high circles for me, Anne dear! I must say I feel a slight reflected glory when I read in the papers that Mrs. Geoffrey Lymes, wife of the well-known play-wright, was amongst the Duchess of Bristol's party at the—wherever it was!

ANNE. (*Her manner changes.*) What paper did you see that in?

GEOFF. I don't remember for the moment!

ANNE. It's too disgraceful—those beastly press-cutting people I belong to never send me anything; can't you remember what paper it was in?

GEOFF. I'm afraid I've forgotten!

ANNE. I'll write to them to-night! Brutes!

GEOFF. Tell me, have you discovered any new

geniuses this week amongst your literary
friends?

ANNE. (*Looks at him.*) No! (*Pauses; speaks
indifferently.*) Letts lunched with me on Tues-
day.

GEOFF. Letts? My word, that's a conquest, if you
like—that's putting it across your friends with
a vengeance!

ANNE. In what way? I don't understand?

GEOFF. The world's great writer—who never is
seen in public, who hates photography almost
as much as the photographer hates him. I call
that a terrific triumph! How did you get him,
Anne?

ANNE. How do you mean, how did I get him?
I wrote and asked him if he would lunch with me.

GEOFF. How many times?

ANNE. Once, of course!

GEOFF. Well, that's marvellous! I was told he
never even answers the first five invitations!
He must have seen some of my plays and said to
himself, 'A clever fellow like that must
obviously have married an interesting woman!
I'll go to lunch!'

ANNE. I don't think he even knew I was married
to you. And when they were talking about you
at lunch, he asked what plays you had written!

GEOFF. Crushed, b'God! Who did you ask to
meet him?

B

ANNE. Lindsay Steele, John Hale, Augustus Gold——

GEOFF. My word, there's a gathering of literary celebrities for you. I wish I were a Highbrow, it's very sad !

ANNE. Yes, Augustus said at lunch what a pity it was you had sold yourself and only wrote for money !

GEOFF. What does he write for, darling ?

ANNE. Not for money, anyway ! (*Smiles.*)

GEOFF. True ! I read his last book, and I have never seen a man write so deliberately to stop the public reading that book than he did ! And I don't believe it was intentional.

ANNE. Darling, are you right to be sarcastic about men like Augustus ?

GEOFF. No, but they shouldn't say I write for money—I do, but they shouldn't say it !

ANNE. Darling, your plays are very amusing and all that, but they are for the moment only, aren't they ? The end of your last play could have been more artistic, but you said, ' Not for you, there wouldn't be a bob in it ! '

GEOFF. I'd just got your bills in for the lunches you had been giving for the fellows who are artistic.

ANNE. (*Angrily.*) That's right—I knew money would come into it sooner or later !

GEOFF. Darling, only a joke!

ANNE. Joke? You meant it; every time I come down here, it's money—money—money—I'm sick of it!

GEOFF. Well, you are extravagant, aren't you?

ANNE. (*Angrily.*) That's right, go on—tell me what the Income Tax is!

GEOFF. For Augustus—threepence!

ANNE. Doesn't posterity mean something?

GEOFF. Undertakers believe in it!

ANNE. I'm sick of it—I travel down in a beastly train every week-end to see you, only to be told how much money I spend, how——

GEOFF. And to tell me how badly I write!

ANNE. Well, everybody knows that!

GEOFF. Darling, I do wish you would remember to talk in your baby language; it means the same, I know, but it sounds so much less arrogant!

ANNE. I'm tired—tired to death of it all! (*Picks up her coat.*) I shall have my dinner in bed!

GEOFF. I'm sorry, I'm afraid you can't do that. My old friend Ernest Melton, whom I hadn't seen for years, and his wife are here for the week-end, they are dressing now.

ANNE. Why should I have to sit up and listen to those bores?

GEOFF. How do you know they are bores; you've

never met them.   I haven't met his wife myself
—I was out when they arrived!

ANNE.   If they're friends of yours, they must
be bores.

GEOFF.   I daresay you are right!   But he has
one attribute that might appeal to you!

ANNE.   I doubt it!

GEOFF.   He'll be a duke one day.

ANNE.   I don't care if he will be two dukes.

(ERNEST *enters*.)

GEOFF.   Ah, my dear Ernest!   You've never met
Anne, have you?

ERNEST.   No, but I've been looking forward to
it so much.   (*Puts out his hand*.)   It's charming
of you to have us for the week-end.

ANNE.   (*Her manner changes; she is charming
and agreeable*.)   I'm delighted—I tried so hard
to get down early so as to be here when you
arrived, but I——

ERNEST.   Please!   Please!

ANNE.   They have given you a comfortable room?

ERNEST.   Charming, thank you so much.

ANNE.   Geoffrey, dear, give Mr. Melton a cocktail.

GEOFF.   (*Takes one off table*.)   Waiting for you,
old friend.

ERNEST.   (*Takes it*.)   Thanks!   (*To* Anne.)
Geoffrey has told you we are very old friends?

ANNE. Indeed he has! You were at Eton and Oxford together, weren't you?

ERNEST. By Jove, it seems remarkable that although we were inseparable both at Eton and Oxford, we have not seen each other for years!

GEOFF. A lot has happened in those years, Ernest, my boy!

ERNEST. We have both married.

GEOFF. We have!

ERNEST. And you have made a great success of life!

GEOFF. I wouldn't say a great success, I——

ERNEST. Nonsense. What is it like to be married to a literary swell like Geoffrey, Mrs. Lymes?

GEOFF. What is it like, darling?

ANNE. One is very proud of him, Mr. Melton.

ERNEST. I'm sure you are! When I was abroad and I read of Geoffrey in the papers, I used to boast that he was my greatest friend. The number of people who wanted to know him was quite flattering to me.

GEOFF. I hope you are staying with us for some time, Ernest?

ERNEST. (*Laughs.*) Just the same feller. Not altered a bit. I congratulate you on having married the best fellow in the world, Mrs. Lymes.

GEOFF. She knows it, old friend, don't you, darling?

ERNEST. I'm sure she does. What a jolly canary!

ANNE. Geoffrey, you naughty man, what is it doing on the table?

GEOFF. I've been trying to persuade the stupid ass that he has more to sing about than most people. Oh, I'm so sorry, Anne, but this telegram came for you just before you arrived.

ANNE. (*Takes it.*) Oh, this is wonderful—but I'm afraid it means the poor darling can't get here until nearly nine. Do you mind very much dining as late as that?

ERNEST. Not in the least.

GEOFF. Who's coming, darling?

ANNE. Russiloff! Ring the—no, I'll tell them as I go out! (*To* ERNEST.) Do ask your wife to be an angel and not mind.

ERNEST. Of course she won't.

ANNE. (*Smiles at him.*) Au revoir. Do ask for anything you want, won't you?

(ERNEST *opens the door for* ANNE.)

ERNEST. I will, indeed!

(*Exit* ANNE.)

ERNEST. Charming, Geoffrey, charming!

GEOFF. She can be the most charming woman in the world, Ernest.

ERNEST. I'm delighted my old friend has been so wise and so lucky in his choice.

GEOFF. I don't believe I deserve it.

ERNEST. I differ. But it doesn't always follow that people get what they deserve.

GEOFF. If I have got what I deserve, I can think of nothing that I have ever done that deserves my getting it.

ERNEST. Frankly, I was a little nervous of meeting her ; one reads in the papers of all the great people she entertains, and of course every one has told me how clever she is.

GEOFF. Brilliant ! But you needn't have been the least nervous ; she hides it even more brilliantly.

ERNEST. Like all really clever people. She's charming ! Forgive my ignorance, Geoffrey, but who is Russiloff ?

GEOFF. Not a notion ! But you can take it from me he's a genius.

ERNEST. Really ?

GEOFF. Anne is a perfect demon at discovering them ; a genius has only to pop his head out of the window, and Anne has got him to lunch the next day.

ERNEST. Really ? Really ? You must find meeting them very helpful to you in your work ?

GEOFF. Ernest, I don't ! You see, I only write for money, and Anne's friends only write for art. I don't believe two per cent. of them would know a pound note from a ten-shilling one.   They are above such things.

ERNEST.   Really ?

GEOFF.   In fact, in the circle in which Anne lives, to reach more than a hundred people signifies failure.

ERNEST.   Really ?   How interesting.

GEOFF.   Your wife is artistic, too, Ernest ?

ERNEST.   No, Geoffrey, she isn't !

GEOFF.   (*To canary.*)   Listen; you might hear something.   (*To* ERNEST.)   She's a sports girl, eh ?

ERNEST.   No, Geoffrey, she isn't.

GEOFF.   (*Nodding at cage.*)   But you are very happy, old friend ?

ERNEST.   I am happy, Geoffrey.

GEOFF.   (*Makes grimace at canary.*)   I'm glad.

ERNEST.   It is very un-English, I know, and against all the teachings of Eton and Oxford to discuss one's wife in other than a favourable way——

GEOFF.   I imagine the only exception both those institutions would make would be an old friend.

ERNEST.   I feel that myself.   And if your married life was, shall we say, not quite what you hoped it would be, you would confide in me ?

GEOFF.   I should consider it my duty to, Ernest. (*Winks at canary.*)

ERNEST. I agree. It's a long story!

GEOFF. Not in the way I hope you will tell it, old friend! (*Moves canary nearer.*)

ERNEST. Why do you keep moving that bird?

GEOFF. I'm always hoping that something might make him sing! Sorry. Go on, Ernest!

ERNEST. Very well. When we left Oxford, conditions, you remember, separated us. You to your work, and I to carry on the traditions of an English gentleman. Hating it, I shot! Fearing it, I hunted! Bored, I raced. But always conscious I was doing the right thing.

GEOFF. I'm sure.

ERNEST. Then to complete my education, I acquired the Bohemian spirit.

GEOFF. What does that mean?

ERNEST. You know! Taking a lady of the streets to dine at an hotel where your relations were dining. One was always expected to do something next!

GEOFF. Naturally!

ERNEST. Buying two front stalls for the entire run of a musical play.

GEOFF. You didn't use them?

ERNEST. I was always late. And then after the play, the fun of going around to the actresses' dressing-rooms and calling them by their Christian names.

GEOFF. What a fool I am, I never thought of doing that!

ERNEST.   And it was in one of those rooms I met Elma.

GEOFF.   Good!

ERNEST.   I was fascinated by her ; entirely unlike the women of my own class, she was gay—she was jolly!   I took her to supper—I told her some of the things I had done in my life.   How amused she was!

GEOFF.   That I'm sure of!

ERNEST.   And then—I drove her home in a taxi!

GEOFF.   (*Draws his chair up*.)   Now then!

ERNEST.   Not meaning anything—on my honour, with no ulterior motive—just carrying on the traditions of an English gentleman, as it were— I was fresh!

GEOFF.   Good!

ERNEST.   In a flash I knew I had made a mistake. Removing my arms, we drove in silence.   I was conscious that whatever I said would be wrong! It was the longest drive I ever remember.   She lived at a place called Streatham ; I think it is somewhere near Eastbourne.

GEOFF.   That's right.

ERNEST.   Reaching her house, she got out, I jumped after her—it was obvious she had been crying—without saying good night or anything, she banged the door in my face!   And then I started my long drive back!

GEOFF.   Go on!

ERNEST.   I realised what I had done—I had hurt

a woman—good as our education is, Geoffrey, it is faulty. I remember my father telling me ' Have fun with the girls, Ernest, my boy, but always play the game.' How the hell you can do both has always defeated me. I wish he had lived, I would have liked to have asked him what he meant !

GEOFF. He meant, never interfere in a woman's life, unless you are a great friend of her husband's.

ERNEST. Possibly ! The next morning I wrote her a generous apology and some flowers ! That night I was in my seat as the curtain rose— but never once did she look—I sent a message to ask her to speak to me—(*Shakes his head*)— she was sorry, she was engaged. In despair, I rushed to the room of the leading man, who was famous for persuading young chorus-girls to go out to supper with old men of old families— he failed ! He told me in confidence it was one of the first failures he had ever been connected with ! He even went as far as to say it put his knighthood back two years. The next morning at eight o'clock I took my courage in both hands and went to Streatham.

GEOFF. Good !

ERNEST. I asked to see her—the maid returned and said she was sorry but she was out. I waited an hour—to be told she had been in all the time. Where do you think she was ?

GEOFF. Where ?

ERNEST. In the garden, gardening !

GEOFF. No !

ERNEST. Yes ! With my own eyes I saw her. Geoffrey, who would have expected to find a chorus girl gardening at nine in the morning ?

GEOFF. Only another chorus-girl !

ERNEST. After a long time she forgave me. And nightly I drove her home to Streatham. Have you ever driven a beautiful but good woman home to Streatham with any frequency, Geoffrey ?

GEOFF. No.

ERNEST. Then you don't know what suffering is. All the forces that Nature possesses are at work against you ! A beautiful face, a divine figure, sweet-smelling scent. A combination of things that even in the darkness show you clearly your slippers by the fireside ; above the rattle of the taxi, the noise of the 'buses, you hear distinctly the patter of little feet ; and although your mind and your imagination are working at their best, your arms remain paralysed, conscious that they are in the presence of a good woman.

GEOFF. (*Wipes his forehead.*) My dear fellow !

ERNEST. Each night I determined to triumph over nature—to fight and conquer her—be just a friend—but each night I failed—so like millions and millions of men before me—I accepted the philosophy that although you cannot control the thoughts that come into your mind—you can at all events legalise them !

GEOFF. And she accepted you?

ERNEST. Yes. Conscious of the difference in our social position, she insisted that in the event of my family wishing the marriage to be postponed for six months or a year, I would agree.

GEOFF. Charming of her.

ERNEST. So to my father, who had regularly told me for twenty-five years that ' Whenever you are in trouble, my boy, come to your old father,' I went. Before I was half-way through the story he called me a bloody fool and my fiancée a whore—with the result we were married in a fortnight.

GEOFF. (*Nods his head.*) Quite! Quite!

ERNEST. But I defy you to show me any man who was happier than I during the first six months of our marriage!

GEOFF. (*To canary.*) That's a long time!

ERNEST. It was perfect! Then for some inexplicable reason it all seemed to change. Our first serious quarrel was about the life of a bee!

GEOFF. Why?

ERNEST. I was listening to it on the wireless— determined to be master in my own house, I refused to take it off! Geoffrey, although there were some Americans in the last play she was in, nothing excuses the reflection she passed on my mother through me that night!

GEOFF. (*Smiles.*) She didn't mean it literally, old friend!

ERNEST. That's what she said—nevertheless, it was inexcusable! Soon I discovered she was without social ambition!

GEOFF. And she was on the stage? That's odd!

ERNEST. One night I introduced her to a cousin of mine, the Duchess of Bristol, and I admit her manner to Elma was a little haughty—but can anything excuse Elma saying to her, 'Do come nearer, I don't smell nearly so bad close.'

GEOFF. (*Delighted.*) She didn't!

ERNEST. I tell you she did!

GEOFF. Well, well, well!

ERNEST. Her simplicity of nature, her inability not to speak her thoughts aloud, ruined my career finally in the Army!

GEOFF. No! How?

ERNEST. I asked a distinguished General, whose influence might have been invaluable to me, to dine with us. I consider it was her duty to listen to his long stories—think of my horror when she stopped him in the middle of one of his longest and said, 'General, as it is very evident there will not be another war in your lifetime—wouldn't it be more patriotic of you to leave the Army and join the chestnut trade!'

GEOFF. (*Delighted.*) She didn't—no—you're making it up!

ERNEST. I tell you I'm not!

GEOFF. What happened?

ERNEST. With soldierly fortitude, he controlled

his angry blood from rising further than his neck. (*Pause.*) Three weeks afterwards, without my regiment, I was ordered to China.

GEOFF. I see!

ERNEST. And there it was the same—men of importance who could discuss the old days of the Army and Navy bored her—she was intolerant of convention ; ultimately our only friend was the manager of a provision store—her excuse was he made her laugh !

GEOFF. A provision store ? In what odd places one finds rare things !

ERNEST. Dissatisfied—a man with no future—I sent in my papers and returned to England. But to what, Geoffrey ?

GEOFF. What do you mean, old friend, I don't quite understand ?

ERNEST. What is our life to be ? Who are our friends to be ?

GEOFF. Well, that's up to you, surely ?

ERNEST. Up to me ? I, who love edifying conversation, who would like to find at my table men of distinction, poets, writers, men with a breadth of vision—the dismissal of pettiness— narrowness—the——

GEOFF. Are you expecting to find these qualities amongst writers ?

ERNEST. Certainly !

GEOFF. I see ! I see ! Well, if the food and the

listening are good you'll have no difficulty in getting them!

ERNEST. But do you suppose if Elma didn't understand, or agree with what they were saying, she would keep quiet? No, Geoffrey, they would never come again!

GEOFF. I must say I am longing to meet your wife, Ernest!

ERNEST. Ah, she has a heart of gold, and all that is wrong with our marriage is, we have not the same tastes. Without the least reflection against Elma, I wish she were like your wife, Geoff!

GEOFF. (*To* CANARY.) Cracked! (*To* ERNEST.) Old friend, perhaps your lawyer could——

ERNEST. Geoff! I belong to the old school who believe that having made your bed, you must lie in it with the woman you made it for.

GEOFF. Times have changed since you made that bed, old friend.

ERNEST. Not for me. Besides, if Elma had the least suspicion I was not completely happy, it would break her heart.

GEOFF. That makes it difficult!

ERNEST. No! I must train myself to like managers of provision stores and such-like! I am hoping very much she will like you, Geoff!

GEOFF. I have a feeling I shall like her, Ernest.

(ELMA *enters.*)

ERNEST. (*Walks to her.*) Darling, this is my dear friend Geoff, whom I have talked to you about so often.

GEOFF. I can't tell you how delighted I am to meet you !

ELMA. (*Smiles.*) Thank you so much !

GEOFF. Where would you like to sit ?

ELMA. Here, if I may. (*Sits down.*)

ERNEST. We have just been talking about the old days, darling !

ELMA. I knew you had, Ernest ! (*To* GEOFFREY.) You were at Harrow and Cambridge with Ernest, weren't you ?

(GEOFFREY *laughs.*)

ERNEST. Really, darling—if I have told you once, I have told you a thousand times—Eton and Oxford.

ELMA. I'm sorry, I'd forgotten, but I know it was some of those places !

(GEOFFREY *is very amused, and gathers she is having fun with* ERNEST, *who is quite unaware of it.*)

ERNEST. (*Almost indignantly.*) Some of those places ! Really, Elma !

ELMA. Ernest, dear, don't be such a snob about your schools ; I went to a University at Streatham, but if people forget and call it Putney, I don't get excited !

c

ERNEST.   Hardly the same, darling ; is it, Geoff ?

GEOFF.   The results seem excellent in your wife's case !   A cocktail, Mrs. Melton ?

ELMA.   (*Pauses.*)   May I, Ernest ?

ERNEST.   If you would like one, dear !

ELMA.   You know I would like one, but may I have one, darling ?

GEOFF.   Are they bad for your health ?

ELMA.   No, good for it !   But they make me a little bright sometimes, and when I get bright, Ernest gets worried !

ERNEST.   Really, darling, Geoff will think I beat you !

ELMA.   Oh, no, he won't   (*To* GEOFFREY.)   He's divine to me !

GEOFF.   Of course !

ELMA.   (*Holds up cocktail.*)   I love my little Ernest !

(ERNEST *laughs nervously.*)

Have I said the wrong thing, darling ?

ERNEST.   No, darling—but perhaps it's a little embarrassing for Geoffrey.

GEOFF.   The reverse—I find it most attractive !

ERNEST.   What a charming room, Geoff !

GEOFF.   I'm glad you like it !

ERNEST.   Charming taste, don't you think, darling ?

ELMA.   (*Looks round.*)   I think it's wonderful !

ERNEST. Your wife is responsible for it, Geoffrey ; it's no good—I know it.

GEOFF. My wife is entirely responsible for it, Ernest.

ERNEST. You will like her so much, dear !

ELMA. Yes, dear—I—I—only hope she will like me !

ERNEST. Of course she will ! I'm hoping very much that you will be the greatest of friends—don't you, Geoff ?

GEOFF. I can think of nothing I should like so much !

(ANNE *enters. She almost rushes into the room. Her brightness and forced gaiety is almost offensive.*)

ANNE. Here you all are ! I'm so sorry, so terribly sorry ! (*Puts out her hand to* ELMA.) How do you do ? So sweet of you both to come for the week-end. I've been looking forward to meeting you so much !

ERNEST. So have we—haven't we, darling ?

ELMA. We've—we've talked of nothing else !

ANNE. Sweet ! Has that wicked Geoffrey given you a cocktail ?

GEOFF. Yes, darling !

ANNE. (*To* ELMA.) Do tell me you're not angry with me for having another guest who's making dinner a half an hour late ?

ELMA. No !

ANNE. Horrid, careless man, hasn't a notion of the ordinary ways of society, probably go fast asleep in the train and never arrive at all !

ERNEST. (*Endeavours to be amused.*) I say, what fun to be like that. (*To* ELMA.) Don't you think so, darling ?

ELMA. (*Obviously fails to see any humour.*) Yes, dear !

ERNEST. I was just saying, as you came in, in what perfect taste you have decorated this room !

ANNE. Laffinson did it. (*Turning to* ELMA.) You know his work ?

(ELMA *looks blankly at her.* ANNE *turns to* ERNEST.)

ERNEST. Laffinson ? I know his name, of course, but——

(ELMA *looks at him.*)

ANNE. Quite mad ; if you didn't pander to the brute, quite capable of leaving you with the room half finished ! Geoffrey, where's the rug for the piano ?

GEOFF. Oh, I—I spilt some ink on it, and I sent it to the cleaners !

(ANNE *pats him : he tries not to be irritable.*)

ANNE. How brutal ! You're a naughty, naughty man ! And to punish you, the moment it comes back, you'll find your little wife will take it to her house in London !

GEOFF. I'll ask the cleaners to send it to you direct!

ANNE. Nonsense! I—I wouldn't dream of taking it from my sweet little man! Of course, dear Mrs. Melton, you were on the stage, weren't you?

ELMA. I was!

ANNE. How thrilling! Do tell me about it! I've always longed to hear what goes on in the theatre!

GEOFF. Anne, dear, Mrs. Melton left the stage some time ago, and I don't suppose——

ANNE. Be quiet, Geoffrey; I must know what goes on in the theatre! You don't mind telling me, do you, Mrs. Melton?

ELMA. Not at all! What is it you actually want to know?

ERNEST. (*In a pacifying manner.*) You know, dear——

ELMA. I don't know, or I wouldn't have asked!

ANNE. Everything! Did you play a part?

ELMA. I married my little Ernest!

ANNE. How thrilling! I must know all the terrible things that happen in a musical play. Do tell me!

ELMA. Well, you've got to be at the theatre half an hour before the play begins; you've got to stay there until it's over—and on Wednesdays and Saturdays you have to do it twice!

ANNE.   Oh ! Is that all ?   How disappointing !
Is that really all ?

ELMA.   Occasionally a man comes round and offers
a suggestion that would make it impossible for
you to know his wife—but after all, that happens
everywhere, doesn't it ?

ANNE.   (*Laughs.*) How sweet ! I must tell
Augustus that—he'll simply adore it ! You
like Augustus Gold's books ?

(ELMA *has obviously never heard of him.*)

(ANNE *looks inquiringly at* ERNEST.)

You do ?

ERNEST.   Oh, indeed I do, indeed I do ! (*To*
ELMA, *excitedly.*) You know, darling, I gave you
one of his books two days ago—' Marigold ' !

ANNE.   (*To* ELMA.) Didn't you simply love it,
Mrs. Melton ?

ELMA.   (*Shakes her head.*) No !

ERNEST.   (*Anxiously.*) But, darling, surely
you——

ANNE.   (*Laughs almost contemptuously.*) But how
amusing—do tell us in your own way what you
thought of it !

ELMA.   I thought it the most awful muck that has
ever been printed !

ANNE.   Awful what ?

GEOFF.   Muck !

ANNE.   (*Almost contemptuously, laughs in a forced
manner.*)   How terribly interesting, poor Augus-

tus ! One of our greatest writers ! Perhaps
you didn't understand it, Mrs. Melton ?

ELMA.   Perhaps that is what it was !

ANNE.   I'm sure that is what it was ! It is a
passionate plea for the freedom of women, a
demand that they should be free people in mind
and body—it's the modern school, Mrs. Melton !

ELMA.   I wouldn't call it modern—nearly every
nice old gentleman who drove me home in a taxi
ten years ago tried to tell me about it !

GEOFF.   (*Laughs.*) I say, that's—(*Laughs—he
appears to be unable to control himself from
laughing.*)

ANNE.   You have amused Geoffrey, anyway, Mrs.
Melton.   Oh, do stop, Geoffrey !

GEOFF.   Sorry !

ERNEST.   (*Who has been nervously trying to inter-
rupt all the time.*)   Anyway, I hope Geoff will
make us laugh on Wednesday night ; we've got
seats for your play, old feller !

ELMA.   And I am looking forward to it—every one
tells me it's splendid !

GEOFF.   I'm so glad.

ERNEST.   (*To* ANNE.)   You like it very much, I'm
sure, Mrs. Lymes ?

ANNE.   Terribly !   It's awfully good !   (*Sighs.*)
Oh, dear !   I do wish Geoffrey would open the
window sometimes.

ERNEST.   (*Quickly.*)   Oh, allow me— (*Starts to
walk to window.*)

GEOFF.   Not that window, old friend !

ERNEST. Sorry !   Which one ?

GEOFF.   A spiritual window.   Anne means open-
ing the window that lets in great thoughts,
helpful tit-bits, etc.

ERNEST.   Oh, sorry!   I thought for the moment—

> (ELMA *laughs, though she makes every endeavour
>   not to.*)

(*Angrily.*)   Please stop laughing, Elma—what is
there funny about it ?

ELMA.   Sorry, darling !

> (GEOFFREY *starts to laugh.*)

ANNE.   (*Frigidly.*)   Stop, Geoffrey !   (*To* ERNEST.)
You must bring your wife to stay with us often ;
she evidently makes Geoffrey laugh, and it is so
good for him.

GEOFF.   Sorry !

> (*There is a pause.*)

Who would like another cocktail ?

ERNEST.   (*Angrily.*)   Not for me, thank you !

GEOFF.   (*To* ELMA.)   You ?

ELMA.   (*Shakes her head.*)   No, thank you.

GEOFF.   Anne ?

ANNE.   (*Snaps.*)   No !

GEOFF.   (*Pause.*)   Even if your friend is punctual,
darling, he can't be here for another twenty
minutes.   Must we really wait for him ?

ANNE. I have put dinner back half an hour! *You* don't mind, do you, Mrs. Melton?

ELMA. Not in the least!

ERNEST. Frankly, I prefer dining late!

ANNE. What a charming guest! I'm so glad that you're fond of reading.

ERNEST. I almost prefer it to anything!

ANNE. That's delightful! I have quite a unique collection of books in my London house, and when you come to lunch with me one day I must show them to you.

ERNEST. I should like that more than I can tell you!

GEOFF. You haven't an altogether bad collection here, Anne, darling!

ANNE. It's nothing like—but it is really a very attractive room. I think you would like it. Do come, I'll show it to you!

ERNEST. I'd like that very much.

ANNE. (*To* ELMA.) It would bore you to look at books, wouldn't it, Mrs. Melton? No, you stay here and make Geoffrey laugh.

(ERNEST *opens door for* ANNE.)

(*They exeunt.*)

(*Pause.*)

ELMA. Would you do something for me?

GEOFF. Anything in the world!

ELMA. Go and send me a telegram saying my mother is dying and I must come home at once!

GEOFF. (*Laughs.*) Why?

ELMA. I'm miserable—I've made such a mess of it again!

GEOFF. Nonsense!

ELMA. I have—your wife can't bear me—Ernest is miserable——

GEOFF. Don't talk such rubbish!

ELMA. It's all Ernest's fault—he is always so certain that I'm going to do the wrong thing, that I get so nervous I do it! I'll catch it to-night when I go to bed!

GEOFF. What for, in Heaven's name?

ELMA. 'Why did you say you didn't like "Marigold"?—why didn't you tell them some amusing things about the theatre—why did you laugh and make me look a fool?' Why didn't I do this—why didn't I do that—oh, why haven't I the courage to just stay at home and grow fat?

GEOFF. (*Laughs.*) I hope you will do nothing of the sort—I hope you will come here often!

ELMA. (*Shakes her head.*) He's so stupid—he'd love to go away and visit his friends alone and be a pompous boy—but nothing will make him! It's the old story, I suppose, of married life!

GEOFF. In what way?

ELMA. If he went without me, he'd be miserable all the time because he would think he'd treated me badly—and people might say we are not getting on—so he makes me come with him—

then I ruin the party ! So either way he catches it, poor darling !

GEOFF. I know !

ELMA. I'm not sure married life isn't worse for men than it is for women—after all, an unhappy married woman can go to bed with a couple of boiled eggs and a detective story—and have a grand time—but a man can't, so he won't believe it !

GEOFF. There's a good deal in that !

ELMA. Oh, if they would stop bothering about making divorce easy—but marriage so difficult —what a happy place this world would be !

GEOFF. How do you suggest that could be done ?

ELMA. I don't know. All I know is you go to a Judge for a certificate when the damage is done, instead of having to go before him and convince him that there is a reasonable chance of happiness before it begins !

GEOFF. For example ! What would have happened in your case ?

ELMA. The Judge would have said—' Young woman, you are suffering like thousands of women before you from the glamour of an engagement—a not too attractive home—a modest fear that no other man will ask you ! Certificate not granted—come back in a year's time ! '

GEOFF. Then in the greatest indignation you would live together ?

ELMA. Well, you do that if you marry, don't
you ?

GEOFF. Yes, but——

ELMA. And if it's a failure, you go on living
like that !

GEOFF. Quite so ! Then I take it if the first
man is wrong you go on to another !

ELMA. Perhaps a third ! Why not ? Nobody
says anything if a woman loses two of her
husbands and marries a third ! They call her
a good old sport, and God bless her !

GEOFF. But there are the children to be
considered !

ELMA. Isn't it wonderful how these little ones
always come to our aid in our final hypocrisy ?

GEOFF. True ! True !

ELMA. Well, it's all very difficult. Anyway, in
my case I know it's a failure—darling that he
is, Ernest has never really left Eton and Oxford
—at heart, though he says he doesn't, he loves
his old pompous relatives—it irritates him to
death that they don't like me—and irritates
him more when they patronise me—so the poor
darling hasn't one minute's peace of mind !
It was very wrong of me ! I oughtn't to have
married the feller——

GEOFF. I think you're being very modest again !

ELMA. Not at all ! He should have married
some nice woman who, hating it, would have
sat for hours on an uncomfortable shooting

stick watching him shoot—who would have loved giving little dinner-parties to dull people —who would have an engagement book full up to the brim a fortnight ahead—he would adore that—but as I can't do that for him, it's my duty to look for a nice suitable woman who can.

GEOFF. And when you have found her?

ELMA. I shall leave him, of course!

GEOFF. I applaud your unusual consideration! But I'm afraid you'll fail to accomplish it.

ELMA. Why?

GEOFF. Even if he wanted to, and I'm sure he doesn't, Ernest is the type that ' having once made your bed you must lie on it! '

ELMA. Nonsense! In six months I would be merely an incident of his youthful impulse!

GEOFF. In less than six months I hope he'd realise what a fool he was to let you go!

ELMA. (*Looks at* GEOFFREY.) Thank you!

GEOFF. I mean it.

ELMA. Anyway, even if you're right, and I don't think that you are—only experience would ever make Ernest realise it!

GEOFF. If he ever leaves you, I hope he'll marry some woman who makes his life such hell he'll come back to you on his knees asking to be taken back!

ELMA. (*Smiles.*) What fun that would be! I'd give anything to see Ernest on his knees asking to be taken back. Six months with a woman that he wishes so much I was like, might make a really nice man of Ernest !

GEOFF.   Would you take him back ?

ELMA.   If he were very sad and miserable—I'm such a fat, easy-going lump—I don't know. Would you ever marry again ?

GEOFF.   I ?   Do you know, I have never thought about it—but now that I do, I don't believe I would.   There may be another woman like Anne in the world, but I am not prepared to risk it !

ELMA.   (*Looks at him.*)   You must be great fun if one ever got to know you better !

GEOFF.   I don't know about the fun—but I hope you'll know me better.

ELMA.   I'm going to do my best !

(ERNEST *enters.*)

ERNEST.   Geoff, old feller !   (*Laughs.*)   I wouldn't be you for a good deal !

GEOFF.   (*Smiles.*)   Be fair, Ernest, give Anne a chance, you've only been with her five minutes !

ERNEST.   You know that I didn't mean that !

GEOFF.   (*Pats* ERNEST *on the back.*)   I'm glad.

ERNEST.   (*Laughs.*)   Stupid old ass !   What I was going to tell you was, you have been lending a lot of your wife's books !

GEOFF.   By Jove, so I have !   What bad luck— she only goes into her library once a year !

ERNEST. And she's waiting to tell you what she thinks about it !

GEOFF. (*With meaning.*) I know !

ERNEST. Oh, by the way, darling, Anne—(*laughs*) —your wife has insisted on my calling her ' Anne,' Geoff !

GEOFF. Good ! Now I can call your wife Elma !

ELMA. Do, Geoffrey !

GEOFF. You were saying something ?

ERNEST. Oh—she has asked us to lunch on Wednesday to meet—I have forgotten his name for the moment—some great Russian writer !

GEOFF. You're lucky ! The only times I have been asked, they all spoke English ! Anyway, I am not nearly so concerned about lunch on Wednesday as I am about dinner to-night. (*To* ERNEST.) You're a rotten guest ; if you said honestly ' Yes, I am hungry,' we wouldn't have to wait for this feller !

ERNEST. What does it matter, waiting a few minutes ?

ANNE. (*Heard off.*) Geoffrey !

GEOFF. Coming, darling !—Charming voice !

(*Exit* GEOFFREY.)

ERNEST. (*Delighted.*) You like Geoff, dear ?

ELMA. He's a pet. Terribly !

ERNEST. I knew you would. I'm so glad ! I must say I'm liking being here most awfully !

ELMA. Has he always had a sweet nature like that ?

ERNEST. Yes, of course—why ? Are you surprised ?

ELMA. I thought, through being married to her, he might have acquired it !

ERNEST. I don't understand.

ELMA. Well, you know—like grief—sometimes it makes the most horrid people kinder and pleasant !

ERNEST. I still don't understand !

ELMA. (*Looks round.*) Her ! Have you ever met a more awful *poseuse* in your life than that woman ?

ERNEST. Are you speaking of Geoffrey's wife ?

ELMA. Oh, be friendly, Ernest, don't always be such a blasted gentleman. I'm not going to shout it about ! Anyway, you should know now what a nice wife you have got !

ERNEST. I don't agree with you at all. I think she is one of the most charming women I have met for years !

ELMA. (*Looks at him.*) You're not serious ?

ERNEST. Certainly I am. She's so amusing, so well read—so clever——

ELMA. Only because you are not, darling.

ERNEST. You'll pardon me, Elma ! You mustn't assume because you do not allow me to talk on serious subjects that I know nothing about them !

ELMA. Sorry, dear !

ERNEST. And I protest against your always suggesting that I'm a fool !

ELMA. I'm sorry.

ERNEST. And I must ask you—I insist—that you do nothing to jeopardize my friendship with Geoffrey and his wife !

ELMA. I promise not to even open my mouth !

ERNEST. (*Angrily.*) There you are—either you always——

ELMA. Darling ! You must choose one of two things—either you must let me say what I like—then we won't be asked any more—or let me keep quiet and let them think you've married a fool !

ERNEST. I can't understand you—one of the most charming—clever——

ELMA. Ernest ! One of these days you'll discover that she is quite the stupidest woman it has pleased God to put on earth. And when you tell me so, I promise not to say—' but didn't I tell you so ? '

ERNEST. I shall never say anything of the sort !

ELMA. Very well, dear.

ERNEST. And when she asks you to lunch on Wednesday, I would like you to accept.

ELMA. Of course I will, dear—and on Wednesday I'll have a headache and then you'll be able to go alone and talk on learned subjects without me being there to cramp your style !

ERNEST. Very well !

D

ELMA.   She's done one thing at all events I have never been able to make you do !

ERNEST.   What ?

ELMA.   She has persuaded you to go somewhere without me, which I've been praying you to do for years !

ERNEST.   Well, the time must come if you won't—

ELMA.   Of course, dear—that's what I have been saying all these years !

(GEOFFREY *enters*.)

GEOFF.   Ernest, my boy, my heartiest congratulations !

ERNEST.   Why ?

GEOFF.   I can't tell you how grateful I am to you !

ERNEST.   But what for ?

GEOFF.   I have at last introduced one of my men friends to the house that Anne likes !

ERNEST.   I'm so glad !

GEOFF.   My dear feller, you don't know what a success you've made with her ! If you had heard what my wife says about your husband, Elma, you would be a very proud woman !

ELMA.   But if you knew what a success your wife has made with Ernest, what a proud man you would be !

GEOFF.   Good—I'm delighted !

ERNEST.   She's charming, Geoff—so easy to get on with—and a brain—phew ! you're a lucky feller !

GEOFF. So are you, old friend !

(ANNE *enters*.)

ANNE. Dear, dear, sweet people—Geoffrey has been so cruel to me about keeping you waiting for dinner like this !

ERNEST. Oh, why ?

ANNE. But if that horrid man isn't here in five minutes we'll start without him !

GEOFF. Good !

ANNE. And the moment the bell rings we'll go straight in—the brute will have to dine just as he is !

GEOFF. Good !

ANNE. (*To piano*.) Oh, my darling, and has no one played you for a whole week ? I'm so sorry to have kept you waiting like this. (*Sits at piano and plays*.)

> (ERNEST *strikes an attitude of knowledge of music*.)

> (GEOFFREY *sits on the arm of* ELMA'S *chair, looking at the ' Sketch.'*)

(*Playing softly*.) But when dear Russiloff comes, I know that you will like him !

ELMA. (*Whispers to* GEOFFREY.) Who is Russiloff ?

GEOFF. (*Whispers*.) I think he's a poet !

ELMA. Oh ! I hoped he was a conjurer !

GEOFF. Not in this house !

ERNEST. Charming ! Charming !

ELMA. (*Whispers to* GEOFFREY.) Look! Ernest has chucked being a literary giant and become a composer!

(GEOFFREY *laughs*.)

ANNE. Making Geoffrey laugh again, you wicked little girl!

ELMA. I was showing him a funny picture in the " Sketch."

ANNE. (*Playing*.) Oh, what a fool I am—of course I'm dining with a relative of yours on Wednesday—Lady Joan—dear woman—insisted on putting me on her committee for canteens for hop-pickers ; we'll meet there, dear Mrs. Melton ?

(GEOFFREY *looks at* ANNE.)

ELMA. No—I'm afraid we won't.

ANNE. I am disappointed! Such a sweet woman —you like her, don't you ?

ELMA. I—!——

ERNEST. (*Changes the conversation*.) What is it that you are playing ?

ANNE. Guess!

ERNEST. Mozart ?

ANNE. Wrong!

ERNEST. Beethoven ?

ANNE. Wrong!

ERNEST. Let me think—Chopin ?

ANNE. Wrong!

ELMA. (*To* GEOFFREY *in a whisper*.) He's trotting them all out, isn't he ?

ANNE. Guess again!

ERNEST. Brahms?

ANNE. No!

ELMA. (*To* GEOFFREY.) Bollinger!

(GEOFFREY *laughs*.)

(ANNE *has been watching* ELMA *and* GEOFFREY *the whole time*.)

ANNE. No; it's by a little man I discovered myself—so clever—such a future! I don't believe you like Lady Joan, dear Mrs. Melton?

(GEOFFREY *appears angry*.)

ELMA. I don't know her!

ANNE. Oh, why is that?

ELMA. I suppose because Ernest didn't marry a hop-picker!

GEOFF. (*Firmly*.) That answer should satisfy everybody.

ANNE. (*Pretending to be innocent*.) But, Geoffrey, darling!

GEOFF. (*Angrily*.) Sufficient!

(DOOR BELL *is heard*.)

ALL. Russiloff!

GEOFF. (*In a whisper to* ANNE.) And just in time!

ANNE. (*To* ERNEST, *curtseys*.) Come along, sir —you shall take me in! (*Takes his arm*.)

(*Exeunt* ANNE *and* ERNEST.)

GEOFF. Shall we emulate the old school, or just be modern ?

ELMA. Oh, let's be both ! (*Takes* GEOFFREY'S *arm.*)

GEOFF. (*Laughs.*) Good !

ELMA. (*Stops.*) Oh !

GEOFF. (*Almost anxiously.*) What is it ?

ELMA. I've just discovered something !

GEOFF. What ?

ELMA. What a wonderful wife your wife would make Ernest !

[CURTAIN]

ACT II

Scene : The same.

Time : A month later.

(Anne *is seated at a piano playing—she keeps looking at* Ernest *anxiously.*)

(Ernest *is sadly looking into space ; his face is resting on his hand.*)

Ernest. (*Shakes his head.*) Beautiful ! So beautiful !

Anne. Ernest, you worry me—there's something the matter—I wish you would tell me !

Ernest. (*Shakes his head.*) I doubt if you searched the world over if you would find any one as unhappy as I am to-day !

Anne. (*Stops playing : comes down.*) But why ?

Ernest. (*Looks at door ; quickly steps back.*) Am I not your husband's best friend ?

Anne. Well ?

Ernest. Have I not accepted his hospitality for a month—and three weeks of it deceived him in every way—have I not even descended to a trick to get him out of his own room that I might tell his wife I loved her !

ANNE. Well, if you won't tell her in front of him, how else can you tell her?

ERNEST. Is it becoming of an old friend to tell an old friend he loves his wife?

ANNE. Yes—if you do!

ERNEST. (*Shakes his head.*) When you yourself are married to another woman!

ANNE. Yes, but you have told me a thousand times that——

ERNEST. I know I have. But what would happen to her if I left her?

ANNE. She'd marry again.

ERNEST. It is not so easy for women like Elma to marry again. No! I despair of ever knowing another happy moment!

ANNE. No one can help falling in love, Ernest.

ERNEST. We all of us can; I should have realised at once when I found myself drawn to you— that such happiness was not for me—I should have remembered my best friend—my wife, and left at once! I don't know why I didn't, it's so unlike me!

ANNE. You're not going to leave me, Ernest?

ERNEST. I have made a decision! To-morrow morning I return to what Elma is pleased to call our home! (*Laughs.*) Home!

ANNE. Oh, why? But I shall see you again?

ERNEST. No!

ANNE. (*Quickly.*) You don't mean that, Ernest

—please say you don't—you're just trying to frighten me!

ERNEST. I never frighten women.

ANNE. Then why did you tell me only two minutes ago that you loved me more——

(ERNEST *looks at door.*)

Oh, it's all right, nobody listens in this house!

ERNEST. You cannot be too certain—I am married to a very unconventional woman!

ANNE. I wish she would hear—tell me you were joking—you don't mean that you will never see me again!

ERNEST. Yes!

ANNE. Ho! then you don't love me!

ERNEST. Sapphire! Sapphire! (*Shakes his head sadly.*)

ANNE. Then why? I know—it's too much trouble—you are frightened what people will say—oh! your wife has been talking to you!

ERNEST. It is none of those things—in the most unexpected way, the most unexpected place— the shame of what I was doing was revealed to me.

ANNE. What do you mean?

ERNEST. Singing happily in my bath this morning —just an abandoned, cheery fellow—thinking of you—thinking how unevenly happiness has been distributed—a vision of what I was doing was thrust upon me—I saw myself as I am and not as I thought I was—my dishonour—my shame—was revealed to me—I was, as it were, held in a vice—that is bad enough—but that is not all—having indulged for some years in the luxury of turning on the hot tap with my big toe—held by my shame—I was unconscious of the heat until it was too late ! It was two of the most unhappy experiences in one that I ever remember ! The only satisfaction I have is—that I deserved it !

ANNE. But I don't love Geoffrey, Ernest !

ERNEST. But he loves you.

ANNE. He doesn't.

ERNEST. (*Shakes his head.*) Again and again he has told me how little he knew of happiness until he married you !

(ANNE *starts.*)

Only last night he said to me—I wish I could tell you, old friend, what Monday morning means to me knowing I won't see Anne again until Friday night !

ANNE. He said that, did he ?

ERNEST. And many similar beautiful things ! Why, only this morning he said——

ANNE. Thank you, I don't want to hear it.

ERNEST. Ah, exactly—— (*Pause.*) Because, like, me you realise how badly we have behaved.

ANNE. (*Wipes her eyes.*) You had no right to make me love you and then—— (*Puts her arms around him.*)

(ERNEST *nervously looks at door, removes them.*) Ernest! Ernest!

ERNEST. Think what his feelings would be if he discovered that I, his best friend, was cheating him like this—I don't believe he'd ever believe in anything again!

ANNE. I believe it's your wife—you don't want to leave her.

ERNEST. Do you think I find it amusing to be continually addressed as Rasputin and Sunny Jim and in front of servants! No! It is only my strong sense of duty that makes me return to what is known as home!

ANNE. With your intelligence what is your life going to be with her, Ernest—think!

ERNEST. (*Shakes his head.*) Ah! Ah!

ANNE. And what is my life going to be if you leave me? Let us tell Geoffrey the truth, please!

ERNEST. And break his heart? As an honourable man, how can I?

ANNE. But only a week ago you said you would like to take me away this minute—rush into a booking-office and say 'two tickets,' and when asked for where—reply 'anywhere and everywhere—my happiness is such that all places look alike!'

ERNEST.   I did say it!   Yes!

ANNE.   You wanted to see the interesting places of the world—the Cathedrals—the museums—places of art—all the things I had taught you to love!

ERNEST.   Don't make it harder than it already is, Sapphire!

ANNE.   Why, Ernest—why not chuck it all—you hate it—you must—let us run to that booking-office!   (*Puts her arms around him.*)

ERNEST.   (*Removes her arms.*)   Please!   Please don't do that, Sapphire, you have no idea how silently Elma can come into a room.   (*Shakes his head.*)

ANNE.   But if you love me?

ERNEST.   Please don't say it so loud, darling—Elma is quite capable of being near that door!

ANNE.   Well, what does it matter if she is—Ernest, I must tell you—I can't bear it!

ERNEST.   One minute!   You must let me look.   (*He walks to door, opens it—a few yards inside it——*)

(ELMA *is walking to the door.*)

(ELMA *enters.*)

ELMA.   Sweet man!   (*To* ANNE.)   He jumps up and opens the door when you leave the room, and he's there ready to open it when you come into it!   What have you been doing?

ERNEST. What have you ?

ELMA. I ? (*Shows letters.*) I have just finished writing ten letters ! (*To* ERNEST.) Good girl ?

ERNEST. Splendid !

> (ANNE *nods her head to* ERNEST, *suggesting that* ELMA *has heard nothing.*)

ELMA. I thought you were both going for a walk ?

ERNEST. We were—but Anne began to play— and I forgot everything !

ELMA. (*To* ANNE.) I am so glad you have taught my little man to like music—

> (ERNEST *shudders.*)

and as soon as we get home, darling, I'll learn to play the pianola. We'll have some lovely evenings !

ERNEST. The pianola is hardly the same as the human touch, Elma !

ELMA. Oh ! the advertisements say it's better. Anyway, I have written to some of the girls in the theatre and told them they must all come to us for the week-ends—some of them sing just lovely—you'll like that, won't you, darling ?

ERNEST. You are not serious when you say that you have written to them, Elma ?

ELMA. Yes ! why not ? Here are the letters ! They are friends of mine, aren't they ? and you like music! (*Pause.*) What's wrong with them?

ERNEST. Nothing at all—but perhaps it won't be very amusing for our other guests to——

ELMA. Nonsense! (*To* ANNE.) You'd like to have a bit of fun when you come to stay with us, wouldn't you?

ANNE. (*Acidly.*) I can't tell you how much I shall like to have a bit of fun!

ELMA. Of course! Won't Millie Gray make her laugh, Ernest?

ERNEST. Do you mean the lady who regularly throws her legs over her head without the slightest provocation?

ELMA. (*Laughs.*) Yes!

ERNEST. I don't think she could make any one laugh!

ELMA. Don't you? Well, she makes me—and she's a great friend of mine—and she's coming for the week-end!

ERNEST. Elma! I must ask you not to post any of those letters until I have discussed it with you!

ELMA. Why not?

ERNEST. Because I say so!

ELMA. (*Shrugs her shoulders.*) All right!

ERNEST. I'm sorry.

ELMA. I said all right.

ANNE. (*Shrugs her shoulders at* ERNEST.) Why don't we continue this outside; it seems so wrong to waste such a lovely afternoon!

ERNEST. True! Yes! Let us do that! You'll come with us, Elma?

ELMA. No, thank you.

ERNEST. It would do you good.

ELMA. Thank you, I am very well.

ANNE. Anyway, I am going out! Don't bother about me, Ernest—I shall only go to the lake!

(ANNE *walks out.*)

ELMA. I wonder if she has any idea how few people there are in the world who would take her out of the lake compared to the number who would push her into it?

ERNEST. Elma! you are speaking of a very great friend of mine—whose guest we are—and I won't have it!

ELMA. All right, Sunny Jim, don't get excited because I don't like your girl friend!

ERNEST. Ho! you promised me faithfully you would refrain from calling me by that most objectionable name!

ELMA. I know I did—but you annoyed me about my friends!

ERNEST. Good God! Haven't you a mind to rise above such people?

ELMA. No! And you are keeping your sweetie waiting—she'll give you such hell if you don't go after her!

ERNEST. What do you mean? It is a matter of

the most profound indifference to Anne if I join her or not !

ELMA. (*Laughs.*)   Don't be silly—can't you take a joke ?

ERNEST.   No one enjoys a joke more than I do—but I don't call that a joke.

ELMA. (*Sits down.*)   Don't be a fool, Ernest—please go—she'll think I have kept you !

ERNEST.   After the suggestion you made, I shall stay here !

ELMA.   Do you want to be called Sunny Jim and Rasputin all through dinner ?   And worse ?

ERNEST.   If you dare, Elma !

ELMA.   If you don't go and join that—oh, I nearly said it—I'll call you names you don't even believe I know !

ERNEST. (*He rises, looks at* ELMA *angrily.*)   Elma, you are impossible !

(*Walks to window.   Exit.*)

(ELMA *rises, walks to window, is looking out of it when* GEOFFREY *enters.*)

GEOFF.   What are you doing at that window ?

ELMA.   I'm not sure that watching love doesn't give one the next best thrill to being loved—anyway, both are very beautiful !

GEOFF.   Elma Melton !   I insist on your coming away from that window at once—to me there is something so despicably unmoral about your

watching your husband making love to my wife
that——

ELMA. Oh, isn't that beautiful—wicked little
woman has tapped him in her baby way with her
fan! Did she put that baby stuff over you
when you were engaged?

GEOFF. Certainly not! It developed after we
were married!

ELMA. Oh! the little minx! She's tapped him
again—and the idiot likes it! Love is very
beautiful!

GEOFF. Mrs. Melton! This must stop—it isn't
healthy—it's indecent—and I insist on your
taking your husband away to-day and never
entering this house again!

ELMA. (*Screams.*) Geoffrey! He's lost his tem-
per—he's tumbled to her!

GEOFF. (*Rises from table—to* ELMA, *in anxiety.*)
What!

ELMA. Oh! No—no—it's all right, he's being a
baby boy too—he lifted his arm as though he
was going to strike her—but it was only to
frighten wicked little girlie! I wish he wouldn't
give me such shocks! (*Looks at* GEOFFREY.)
It gave you a fright, duckie!

GEOFF. It did nothing of the sort.

ELMA. Then what did you rush to the window
for?

GEOFF. It's a man's duty to show some interest

E

if another man threatens to strike his wife, isn't it ?

ELMA. I don't know ! It depends ! Oh ! Look at all the letters I haven't written !

GEOFF. What do you mean ?

ELMA. (*Opens envelope—takes out blank piece of notepaper.*) He thinks I have written to all my old friends and asked them for every week-end—oh ! it was good work !

GEOFF. Elma, really, I——

ELMA. Don't be such a damned humbug !

GEOFF. Humbug ! Sit down there ! I wish to tell you during my career as a playwright I have come in contact both on and off the stage with some desperate characters—but they all fade into insignificance when I think of you !

ELMA. He calls her Sapphire !

GEOFF. (*Eagerly.*) I don't believe it

ELMA. He does, I tell you.

GEOFF. Did you laugh ?

ELMA. Oh, it wasn't in front of me !

GEOFF. Then how do you know ?

ELMA. I overheard by accident.

GEOFF. (*Angrily.*) Your lack of ordinary convention horrifies me.

ELMA. What have I done ?

GEOFF. (*Angrily.*) What haven't you done !

Amongst other things you come into the home
of two married people—and return their hospitality by what—not only taking your host's
wife from him for your husband—but also have
the audacity to ask him to be a party to it !
It's un-English !

ELMA. I'm sorry !

GEOFF. Sorry ? I don't believe such an appalling
suggestion has ever been made in an English
home before !

ELMA. I have only been to two week-end parties
in English houses.

GEOFF. I don't know what you are suggesting,
Elma—and I don't want to know—but I am
certain, whatever the guests did, they had the
decency not to let any one else know what they
were doing !

ELMA. None of the husbands seemed to know !

GEOFF. Exactly !

ELMA. (*Bends over, whispers.*) He wants to rush
into a booking-office, take two tickets for anywhere, and run away with her this afternoon !

GEOFF. (*Eagerly.*) No ! I don't believe it !

ELMA. It's true !

GEOFF. How do you know ?

ELMA. I overheard by accident !

GEOFF. You listened ?

ELMA. (*Looks away.*) I don't know what you
mean ?

GEOFF. (*Angrily.*) This must stop!

ELMA. After all, there is this to be said in his favour, he does love your wife!

GEOFF. The cad! The friend of my schoolboy days! (*Shakes his head.*) What a pretty advertisement for Eton and Oxford!

ELMA. And your wife loves him!

GEOFF. (*Angrily.*) That's a lie! My wife is much too clever to love anybody!

ELMA. Well, she understands him!

GEOFF. Yes! She understands him! But what exactly is my position in all this—am I to sit still and watch the deplorable behaviour of my friend and his wife—under my very eyes watch my home being broken up—and just say nothing!

ELMA. Never turn the hot tap on with your big toe!

GEOFF. I always do!

ELMA. Ernest burnt himself!

GEOFF. (*Eagerly.*) Where?

ELMA. I don't know—we are not on those terms!

GEOFF. Do you mean to tell me he had the audacity to discuss things of such a private nature with my wife?

ELMA. Artistic people are always abandoned!

GEOFF. (*Bends over.*) Elma Melton—you are a very, very bad woman!

ELMA. I know! But if you hadn't told me the other night——

GEOFF. You are not going to refer to that most unfortunate alcoholic observation I made !

ELMA. But you did say it !

GEOFF. What did I say to you after the second glass of champagne that night ?

ELMA. Your wife was the best little woman in the world !

GEOFF. Exactly ! Be good enough to remember that !

ELMA. What did you say after the fourth glass ?

GEOFF. (*Hesitates.*) It was bad champagne !

ELMA. You called me little woman—which annoyed me very much, and said ' that as I was different to any other woman you had ever met ' you didn't mind telling me that your wife could be the most awful bore in the world !

GEOFF. Well, there's nothing very much in that —most men could say that about their wives !

ELMA. When you had finally said no to the brandy—you said that the only thing that prevented you hitting her sometimes was that everybody had told you all your life it was wrong to hit women !

GEOFF. Obviously only a remark !

ELMA. You never meant it ?

GEOFF. Certainly not !

ELMA. Then why did you say to that canary this morning ' Cheer up, Percy, there's a chance of freedom ? '

GEOFF. Ho! ho! You listened—how could you, Elma?

ELMA. (*Indignantly.*) Wouldn't any one listen to a man talking to a canary—mustn't it obviously be something he doesn't want any one else to know?

GEOFF. True! Yes! That's true!

ELMA. Of course!

GEOFF. Elma! It is very evident that there are some people in the world with whom there is nothing to be gained by being dishonest!

ELMA. Well?

GEOFF. So, I'll tell you the truth—I don't like it—but I will! All that I said in alcoholism—I think in sobriety! My wife is a bore—it is as much as I can do to sit in the same house with her without screaming—I crave for my freedom more than for anything else in the world—but I don't like the way I'm going about getting it!

ELMA. What's wrong with it?

GEOFF. I don't say it's wrong—but it's un-English!

ELMA. How would you like it done, then?

GEOFF. I would like them to be going on just as they are now—but you and I apparently unconscious of it—and when it had run its natural course—and they had left us both—for me to be able to say to you in horror 'Had you any idea?' and you to reply indignantly—'Do you suppose if I had known this was going on under my very nose, I would have stayed in your house for one moment? ' In brief, I want to lose my wife but keep my self-respect! I want to be a gentleman!

ELMA. What do you want to be a gentleman for with all your gifts?

GEOFF. I hadn't thought of that—that's true!

ELMA. For goodness' sake leave something for men like Ernest!

GEOFF. That's true, too!

ELMA. Why don't you face it in a big way like your wife has done?

GEOFF. My wife has behaved disgracefully!

ELMA. Magnificently!

GEOFF. What do you say?

ELMA. Listen—for years you have bored her!

GEOFF. (*Starts.*) I—I have bored her? (*Laughs ironically.*) You'll pardon me, Elma Melton! I bore nobody.

ELMA. Congratulations! For years she has craved for social position—what social position has a playwright?

GEOFF. (*Haughtily.*) I am under the impression every one wishes to know him!

ELMA. Don't be ridiculous—he seldom has sex appeal and is rarely amusing—and only a third of the people who see his plays have got enough brains to know any one wrote it!

GEOFF.   How right you are !

ELMA.   She would have had much more chance of
social success if she had married an actor !

GEOFF.   (*Indignantly.*)   Elma ! That I will never
agree with !

ELMA.   If you have only seen them act on the
stage, I agree—but if you have seen them act on
golf courses—entering a restaurant—or wherever
two or three people are gathered together, then
I do not agree !

GEOFF.   It is seldom a man of letters has been so
bitterly humiliated.

ELMA.   And Ernest can provide for all her cravings
—he has money—and one day a great social
position—and he won't bore her any more than
you do—and under our very noses she has
without deceit—without scruple—without com-
promise—honestly set out to catch him—leave
you and take him from me !   Brushing aside my
personal hope and prayer that she will succeed
—she has behaved with such courage and fair-
ness, I hope she gets him ! Personally, I am
going to give her all the help I can !

GEOFF.   I hadn't looked at it in that way—do you
think that I, too, should help her ?

ELMA.   If you have the slightest regard or affection for your wife you certainly will.

GEOFF.   I am devoted to my wife—and I'll prove

it ! Ah ! But what about my position with
Ernest ?

ELMA. What about it ?

GEOFF. Knowing my wife as I do, is it fair to
allow him to rush into this calamity without a
word of warning ? Am I, as it were, being a
cricketer ? That worries me ! If he were a
stranger to me, it would be a different matter—
but to allow the friend of my schoolboy days to
marry my wife without warning—doesn't it
savour to you rather of cheating at cards ?

ELMA. If he marries your wife, it is obvious that
he must have done something to offend nature
so deeply she is determined to be ruthless in her
punishment !

GEOFF. (*Smiles.*) And I will comfort myself in
the knowledge that nature has chosen me to be
one of her chief instruments ! Yes !

ELMA. The time has arrived when we must take
some attitude——

GEOFF. Yes ! I shall immediately ask your
husband what his intentions are ?

ELMA. You'll do nothing of the sort—Ernest at
the moment thinks you're a fool and have no
idea of what is going on—if you disillusion him
he'll remember Eton—Oxford—the Oval— Sand-
wich—run like a hare, taking me with him !

GEOFF. He thinks I am a fool—and that I don't
know, does he ?

ELMA. Ernest is a gentleman! You don't suppose he would be such a cad as to make love to your wife if he thought you knew it?

GEOFF. Elma—I am unable to tell you how much I resent Ernest thinking me a fool—and it was in my mind to let him off and suffer myself—but now it is different—even nature has no idea how far I will go to help her!

ELMA. You'll have to be quick—we are leaving here to-morrow.

GEOFF. Did you overhear why he is leaving?

ELMA. He can't go on cheating his boyhood friend like this any longer! If you discovered him you would never believe in anything again!

GEOFF. That's bad! You don't think he wants to get out of it, do you?

ELMA. Why?

GEOFF. Well, that's usually the stuff they put over when they are getting tired of the lady!

ELMA. How do you know?

(GEOFFREY *shrugs his shoulders.*)

GEOFF. How do you suggest we should begin?

ELMA. When they come in, be nice to Ernest, but say something to your wife that will give her the chance to wipe away the tears that force their way into her eyes——

GEOFF. Nothing would make Anne cry!

ELMA. But Ernest doesn't know that yet!

GEOFF. That's true.

ELMA. And realising the seriousness of the situation, as she does, the least thing will make her cry!

GEOFF. Why?

ELMA. Look at the strong position it puts her in with Ernest—poor little woman who has suffered so much in silence—and it strengthens his position with you so much!

GEOFF. How?

ELMA. Where is the dishonour of taking a woman from a man who makes her cry?

GEOFF. It seems to me he is coming out of this a hell of a feller!—but having discovered he owes me nothing—there's still you!

ELMA. I'll fix him all right! My business is at the psychological moment to burst in and say I know everything!

GEOFF. And then?

ELMA. I have faith in your wife!

GEOFF. Do I know?

ELMA. It comes as the most hideous shock you have ever known?

GEOFF. Yes, that's right! It would never do for me to have ever been even suspicious! No! It is imperative that I must be just a simple, trusting feller. Yes! But tell me this— ethically are we not doing a most disgraceful thing?

ELMA.   Logically, we are behaving splendidly!
If we don't make him marry your wife, what
sort of life is mine going to be—the woman who
stood between him and his happiness—jolly for
me, wouldn't it be?

GEOFF.   (*Looks at* ELMA.) Terrible! In the
event of this ending satisfactorily, what are
you going to do, Elma?

ELMA.   I suppose I had better go home to my
mother!

GEOFF.   Nonsense! Tell your mother to come here
and stay here with us!

ELMA.   I would like that—even if she can't come!

GEOFF.   (*Laughs.*) I'm terribly fond of you,
Elma.

ELMA.   I adore you!

GEOFF.   You don't!

(VOICE *heard* OFF.)

ELMA.   'Ssh! I shall be asleep!

GEOFF.   And I shall be sitting innocently unaware
that all is not well with my domestic life! But
I'll give him hell when I do know!

(ANNE *enters, followed by* ERNEST.)

ANNE.   (*Laughing.*) You're the most ridiculous
person in the world, Ernest!

GEOFF.   No, no, not a word against my dear old
friend!

ERNEST. Thank you, Geoff!

ELMA. (*Wakes up, rubs her eyes.*) I wish you wouldn't make so much noise!

ERNEST. Sorry, darling! You don't mean to tell me you two have been sitting in here on a lovely afternoon like this?

GEOFF. We have! She slept and I read a little —then I thought—how happy one is—a charming house—delightful friends—(*Pause*)—peace of mind! (*Sighs.*) Very, very charming!

ERNEST. I'm ashamed of you both. Anne and I went for a most attractive walk!

ANNE. I took Ernest to the wood and showed him where you work in the summer, Geoffrey.

ERNEST. It was charming. The sun was shining on the hills—the birds were singing—the trees were in blossom—it was all very beautiful.

ELMA. And what was most beautiful of all was that you weren't with your wife.

ERNEST. (*Indignantly.*) That was not my fault, Elma—I asked you to come.

ELMA. Oh, you asked me all right!

ANNE. We both begged you to come.

ERNEST. (*Looks at her—is nervous of what she is going to say next.*) Geoff, old friend, I hope you will think it bad news—but you are losing Elma and myself to-morrow.

GEOFF. Not on your life I'm not! You don't go a day before Monday.

ANNE. That's what I said!

GEOFF. Oh, it doesn't matter what you said— it's what I say!

ANNE. (*Angrily.*) I suppose I may speak in my own house?

GEOFF. I can't stop you—if you mean to.

(ANNE *sinks into chair—endeavours to look as though she is trying not to cry.*)

What's the matter, Anne? (*To* ERNEST.) The old girl's tired! You're looking terribly tired, old girl—you haven't been looking your beautiful self for some time.

ANNE. (*Wipes her eyes.*) You beast!

GEOFF. Good heavens—I don't understand! Have I said anything?

ANNE. (*Crying.*) You meant to be horrid to me— you are always horrid to me.

GEOFF. (*To* ERNEST.) Ernest, as my oldest friend, did I say anything that deserves my wife speaking to me like that?

ERNEST. Well, Geoffrey, frankly, I do think your manner was a little uncalled for.

ELMA. Rot! He said nothing at all.

ANNE. (*Sobbing.*) Oh! Oh!

ERNEST. Elma, be good enough to remember you are a guest in this house.

ELMA. Isn't it about time you remembered it?

GEOFF. Oh, do stop it, Anne—making me out a brute in front of my oldest friend! Making an idiot of yourself like this!

ANNE. There! There! You're always the— the—the same—you're—you're always beastly to me.

GEOFF. Ernest, the truth. Did I say anything that entitles Anne to speak to me like that?

ERNEST. (*Nervously.*) Well——

GEOFF. (*Angrily.*) Did I?

ELMA. Did he?

ERNEST. (*To* ELMA.) Be quiet!

ELMA. How dare you speak to me like that?

ERNEST. (*Nervously.*) I do dare—you have no right to interfere in things that are not your concern.

ELMA. It's as much my concern as it is yours— and if you think just because you are in love with another woman that I am going to stand here——

GEOFF. Elma! You are forgetting yourself! You're being silly.

ELMA. I'm nothing of the sort—I tell you he is in love with another woman——

GEOFF. I do not believe it—I know from what he has told me that he is in love with you.

ELMA. If you weren't a fat-headed——

ERNEST. Elma! Silence! If I am not mistaken, you are about to make a suggestion that you would regret all your life.

ELMA. Yes, I am. I can't stand it any longer—the position I have been put in for weeks, I——

ERNEST. Elma, please—please——

GEOFF. (*Pats* ERNEST *on the back.*) I am sympathetic, old friend—but let us remember that our little Elma is not herself—and——

ELMA. I am myself—and if you weren't a stupid, simple idiot you'd know it.

GEOFF. Know what?

ELMA. That he is in love with your wife!

GEOFF. (*With great anger.*) It's a lie!

ELMA. It's the truth.

ERNEST. Oh, my God—Oh, my God!

GEOFF. (*Walks quickly to* ERNEST.) That is a lie, isn't it, Ernest?

ERNEST. Yes.

GEOFF. (*To* ELMA.) How dare you? How dare you—having upset yourself excuses you—but only a little. (*Pats* ERNEST *on the back.*) Old friend!

ELMA. (*Beside herself with rage.*) Didn't you tell her in this room this afternoon that you loved her more than you could ever love any one?

ERNEST. I did not.

ELMA. You—you—didn't tell her that you would

like to rush into a booking-office and take a ticket for anywhere, as you loved her so much all places looked alike ?

ERNEST. I did not.

ELMA. Do you mean to stand there and tell me that you didn't tell her you had scalded yourself in the bath this morning ?

GEOFF. How dare you ?

ERNEST. (*Starts.*) Oh, I did not !

ELMA. Didn't you kiss her and call her your little Sapphire ?

ERNEST. No, I did not.

ANNE. May I speak ?

ERNEST. No, no, please.

ANNE. Ernest, it is divine of you to protect me like this—and I shall always be grateful to you— but I cannot allow you to do so any longer.

ERNEST. Please, please, Sapphire—Anne !

ANNE. (*To* GEOFFREY.) All that—that—— (*pauses*) Ernest's wife says is true.

GEOFF. (*Horrified.*) No—no—my oldest friend —Eton and Oxford—no, no !

ELMA. (*Aside to* GEOFFREY.) Too much.

ANNE. I'm sorry—but it's true !

GEOFF. I refuse to believe it—you're joking with me, Ernest !

ELMA. Can't you say anything, you Rasputin in the grass !

F

GEOFF.   Silence !

ELMA.   I won't.

GEOFF.   Ernest—tell me it's a joke ! I see it all —the three of you are in league to play this joke on me.

ANNE.   Speak, Ernest.

ERNEST.   (*Looks on the ground.*) No, Geoffrey, it's true.

GEOFF.   It's—(*pauses*) true—you—you—love my wife ?

ERNEST.   Yes.

GEOFF.   And you have told her so ?

ERNEST.   Yes.

GEOFF.   And she loves you ?

ANNE.   Yes.

GEOFF.   I shall never believe in anything again.

ELMA.   Thank heaven you have had the sense to get them both to admit it !

ANNE.   (*To* ELMA.) One thing to me is evident, you were listening at the door.

ELMA.   And another thing is evident—if either of you had any brains you wouldn't have said the things you said to each other with a door !

ERNEST.   Elma, I can never forgive you as long as I live.

ELMA.   And what makes you think that you will ever have the chance to—and let me tell you that anything you have to say to me, say now—because it's your last chance.

ERNEST. I have nothing to say to you.

ELMA. That has been my experience ever since I married you.

GEOFF. (*Holding his head.*) My home broken asunder—and by my best friend! For a playwright, how little I know of life!

ERNEST. What am I to say to you, Geoffrey?

ELMA. Don't ask such stupid questions!

ERNEST. Have you no regard for the seriousness of such a moment as this?

ELMA. None.

ERNEST. Well, kindly leave those of us who have. Geoffrey—I—I—must speak to you.

GEOFF. Ernest—I wish to hear nothing more! I couldn't stand anything more.

ERNEST. But I must—if I could have a few minutes with you alone.

ELMA. No! I'm in this—anything you have to say must be said before me.

ANNE. May I speak?

ERNEST. Please!

ANNE. It is perfectly true, Geoffrey—I love Ernest—I am sorry you have learnt that fact in the way that you have—I wish it could have been told you in a more ordinary way—but the fact remains that you do know it—I am not sorry—I'm glad—at the risk of hurting you more than you are already hurt—I'm happy that you know.

GEOFF. (*Puts his face in his hands.*) Go on.

ANNE. For years I have been unhappy and miserable—perhaps it was not your fault—but for years I have wanted my freedom.

GEOFF. (*Shakes his head.*) Go on.

ANNE. I never intended to like any one else—but these things happen when we least expect them —but now that I do like some one else—and now that you know it—I must tell you it is my intention to leave this house to-night and for ever.

ERNEST. No, no.

GEOFF. Anne! Do you know what you are saying?

ANNE. Yes, Geoffrey.

GEOFF. And you mean it?

ANNE. Yes, Geoffrey.

GEOFF. I don't know what to say!

ERNEST. Could I—would you mind if I said something?

ELMA. Yes, we would.

ANNE. Please, Ernest. (*To* GEOFFREY.) I'm sure Geoffrey agrees that there is nothing else I could do?

GEOFF. Anne! Feeling as you do—bitter as it is for me—there is nothing else that you can do. (*Angrily.*) And I only hope that villain will make you happy!

ELMA. Impossible.

ERNEST. Could I please say something?

GEOFF. No! Having ruined my life—I want to hear nothing from you—or ever see you again. Go.

ELMA. Yes, go and show her where you scald yourself!

ANNE. Be quiet, you vulgar woman.

ELMA. How dare you speak to me like that!

GEOFF. Stop! Under no circumstances will I allow this parting to end in a brawl. I insist that it is conducted with breeding and convention.

ANNE. Thank you, Geoffrey. I'm going to take a few things with me—my maid will remain the night and bring the rest of my things to-morrow, if that is agreeable to you.

GEOFF. Perfectly.

ERNEST. Oh, please—don't let us do anything in a hurry——

GEOFF. Hurry? The moment Anne is ready I expect you to be ready to leave with her!

ERNEST. But——

GEOFF. There are no buts, Melton—I have nothing more to say to you. (*Suddenly.*) You're not going to sit there and tell me you are not prepared to stand by your iniquity!

ANNE. Ernest, there is no obligation for you to come with me unless you want to.

ERNEST. I don't know what you mean, Anne!
Of course I want to, but I must be allowed to
explain to Geoffrey——

ANNE. Very well then—perhaps you would meet
me in the hall in ten minutes! Geoffrey—I'm
sorry if I have hurt you terribly—sorry. (*She
turns and*——)

(*Exit* ANNE.)

ERNEST. (*Anxiously.*) Geoffrey, I—Elma, on
my knees I implore you—I can't leave Geoffrey
like this—I must speak to him!

ELMA. Well, why don't you?

ERNEST. But you would embarrass me—I—
Geoffrey, in memory of the old days—I know
I don't deserve it—in memory of the day when
you jumped in and took me out of the river——

GEOFF. (*Jumps up.*) Did you hear that, Elma
—I saved his life that he might live to ruin mine!

ELMA. You ought to have known!

GEOFF. Yes.

ERNEST. Geoffrey, please, I implore you! I
won't keep you a minute—and I must speak to
you before Anne is ready. I may never see
you again, Geoff.

GEOFF. And do you think I want to ever see
you again? It's more than you deserve, but

I will give you two minutes. (*Walks to* ELMA.) For that time only, would you be good enough to leave us?

ELMA. Very well, if I'm not wanted!

GEOFF. (*Smiles at her.*) But you are wanted.

ELMA. Don't weaken.

GEOFF. Is it likely?

(*Exit* ELMA.)

(*Angrily.*) Well, what have you to say to me?

ERNEST. For God's sake don't speak to me like that, Geoffrey.

GEOFF. Well, how do you expect me to speak to you?

ERNEST. I know I've behaved like a cad—in fact, a much greater cad than you think I have.

GEOFF. I did not ask for details, Melton.

ERNEST. Call me Ernest.

GEOFF. I won't! Come—what is it you wish to say?

ERNEST. I'm shaking so much, could I have a little brandy?

GEOFF. (*Looks at him, hesitates.*) Yes.

ERNEST. (*Walks to sideboard.*) Thank you.

GEOFF. Bring the damn stuff here, I'll have one.

ERNEST. Yes, Geoff. (*He brings the tray, pours out some for* GEOFFREY.) Enough?

GEOFF. No.

(ERNEST *pours out more, gives it to* GEOFFREY. *Then he fills his own glass and sits.*)

(*They look at each other.*)

GEOFF.   I can't drink to your health—but for my wife's sake I hope you will make her a better husband than you have me a friend. (*Drinks.*)

ERNEST.   I realise I cannot make her a worse one, Geoff.

GEOFF.   My God! Do you realise what you have done—you come into the house of your oldest friend—I can't go on—without a thought he trusts you with the best little woman in the world—and you end your visit by telling him that you love her!

ERNEST.   (*Looks round at door.*)   But I don't.

GEOFF.   (*Jumps out of his chair.*)   What do you say?

ERNEST.   That's what I've been wanting to tell you all the time—I don't love her.

GEOFF.   (*Startled out of his life.*)   You—you—don't!

ERNEST.   For ten days I thought I did.

GEOFF.   For ten days! What is your object in telling me this?

ERNEST.   Because you love her—and want her with you.

GEOFF. You are not suggesting to me that you don't want her yourself?

ERNEST. Yes.

GEOFF. Oh, you contemptible blackguard!

ERNEST. I'm not, Geoff.

GEOFF. You're the worst man I have ever known in my life.

ERNEST. But——

GEOFF. You make a woman love you—treat her as a plaything—and the moment it comes to a climax, you're afraid of your conscience—of public opinion. No, you villain—that's not good enough for me—you're dealing with the wrong man. What you have done cannot be undone—leave this room at once and wait for her in the hall.

ERNEST. For God's sake, Geoff!

GEOFF. Go. I can forgive you loving my wife—but I will never forgive you for saying that you don't.

ERNEST. But I don't.

GEOFF. Ho, ho! Didn't you say to her in this room this afternoon that you would like to rush into a booking-office and take her round the world?

ERNEST. Of course! You didn't expect me to be such a cad as to say I didn't want to, do you? One is not without chivalry, I hope.

GEOFF. Chiv . . . you didn't want to take her
for that trip ?

ERNEST. My dear fellow, I'd have hated to.

GEOFF. Melton, if I were a gentleman, I'd knock
you down.

ERNEST. But, Geoff, you don't seem to understand—I'm trying to give her back to you.

GEOFF. Oh, I see that very clearly, but you'll
fail, Melton, you'll fail ! And let me tell you
this, you're provoking me to be a gentleman at
any moment.

ERNEST. I don't understand—I thought you
would be delighted.

GEOFF. At what ?

ERNEST. When I told you I didn't love her.

GEOFF. You callous—you—didn't you hear
my wife say only a minute ago that she loved
you ?

ERNEST. Yes, but she'll get over it in no time.

GEOFF. It's a lie—I know my wife better than you
do—she'll never get over it—it is obvious you
are the only man she has ever loved or ever will
love—if she knew you didn't love her, the
shock would be so great I wouldn't answer for
the consequences. Go to the hall at once.

ERNEST. No, Geoff—you exaggerate—you think
that of her because you are fond of her—but I
know better—in a week I would be merely a
memory.

GEOFF. Let us get to the point, Melton ; answer me this—are you going to marry my wife, or aren't you ?

ERNEST. I'm not going to, Geoff.

GEOFF. For the last time, Melton, are you going to marry my wife, or are you not ?

ERNEST. Geoffrey ! You may strike me—you may maim me, you may stamp on my face—but I will not marry your wife.

GEOFF. Pass me that bottle before I lose control of myself.

ERNEST. May I help myself first ?

GEOFF. No ! What do you want it for ?

ERNEST. I must, Geoffrey—my nerves are terribly upset. (*Helping himself.*)

GEOFF. What about mine ?

ERNEST. I don't know why yours are. You love your wife—and you have got her back !

GEOFF. It must be only the fear that you might successfully retaliate that stops me hitting you. (*Pours himself out brandy.*) Ernest, let me appeal to your better nature—are you—are you prepared to hurt a woman as much as you are threatening to hurt my wife ?

ERNEST. Yes, Geoff——

GEOFF. You, a gentleman by birth, don't mind her thinking you are a cad until the last day of her life ?

ERNEST. No, Geoff.

GEOFF. Ho! A woman that you kissed in this very room this afternoon!

ERNEST. I did not kiss her. At the most it could be described as a chivalrous brush of the forehead.

GEOFF. The same thing to a woman, Ernest.

ERNEST. I assure you not, Geoffrey.

GEOFF. So—so—loving *you*—you expect *me* to take her back?

ERNEST. But I see many advantages in that.

GEOFF. (*Angrily.*) Tell me one.

ERNEST. When she discovers how badly I have behaved—don't you see what a lesson it will be to her—she can appreciate you so much more than she has ever done before. No other man would ever appeal to her again—you'll have her with you for always.

GEOFF. Quick—pass the bottle—I'm going to faint!

ERNEST. Geoffrey, please, you've had three.

GEOFF. And I'm going to have thirty-three. (*Fills up glass.*) You blackguard, Melton, you blackguard! How did you tumble to her?

ERNEST. What do you mean?

GEOFF. You know what I mean—I don't care— poor little Elma will be disappointed, though; it's going to be an awful shock when she discovers she hasn't got rid of you.

ERNEST. What do you mean?

GEOFF. My word, she's a good sort—(*laughs*). We've had some grand laughs at you and Anne during the last three weeks.

ERNEST. You're not telling me you knew all the time? (*Rises.*)

GEOFF. Even Percy, the Canary, knew.

ERNEST. Oh! And you did nothing to stop it!

GEOFF. If you had been married to my wife, and I was trying to take her from you, would you have tried to stop me?

ERNEST. No. (*Sits.*)

GEOFF. Of course not. How did you tumble to Anne, Ernest?

ERNEST. It will be painful, Geoff.

GEOFF. Go on! Go on!

ERNEST. (*Pours himself out another glass.*) When I first met her, Anne swept me off my feet—she discovered qualities in me that I knew I did not possess—she threatened to make me a great man —and generally she surrounded me with an atmosphere that was so unreal, so artificial, that for a little while I was unusually happy.

GEOFF. Go on.

ERNEST. Soon I discovered she was a bigger fake than she was making me—it was a great shock, Geoffrey.

GEOFF. Horrible.

ERNEST. And then she seemed to forget that my name was Ernest, and called me Toosy Wootsy !

GEOFF. And playfully hit you with her fan.

ERNEST. (*Angrily—rising.*) Sometimes I could have taken that fan from her and given her such a one that——

GEOFF. Same here. (*Passes the bottle.*)

(*They both help themselves.*)

ERNEST. When that feller you had to dinner the other night said England was effete, I nearly rose and said : ' How the hell can that be when Geoff has stuck this woman for six years ? '

GEOFF. Six and a half !

ERNEST. Geoff, please don't think me impertinent, but how did you stand it ?

GEOFF. God knows !

ERNEST. What are you going to do about it !

GEOFF. Now that you have failed me, what can I do ? When you and Elma leave, couldn't I come with you ? (*Laughs.*)

ERNEST. Under the circumstances, wouldn't that be a little unmoral ?

GEOFF. I don't know. There are a great many more men going round the world with a friend they don't know than with a friend they do. Let's have some champagne.

ERNEST. Yes.

GEOFF. No—it means waiting—let's go on with this !

ERNEST. You're not angry with me ?

GEOFF. Angry with you—I'm proud of you !

ERNEST. And you don't think I ought to marry your wife ?

GEOFF. I'd have you put in a home if you tried !

ERNEST. Geoff—you are a good feller !

GEOFF. So are you !

ERNEST. What do you think I should say to Anne ?

GEOFF. I'll tell you all the things I think about her—and you repeat them to her as your own !

ERNEST. It's going to be a hateful scene, Geoffrey !

GEOFF. Write to her—why do you want to go and get yourself all upset because of my wife— write to her—tear the address off the note-paper so that she doesn't know where to send you an answer !

ERNEST. Isn't that rather a caddish thing, not to face one's responsibilities in life ?

GEOFF. No—don't be a fool ! If you saw her, she'll get you !

ERNEST. I hadn't thought of that !

GEOFF. I had—you stand by me, dear old friend !

ERNEST. Geoff—you are a good feller !

GEOFF. Mind you, I have one thing against you—

I can never forgive you for wanting to leave a charming woman like Elma !

ERNEST. Geoff, I could cry with shame when I think of the way I've treated her. This I would like to say in your wife's favour, if it hadn't been for her, I should never have known what a treasure Elma was !

GEOFF. Quite right. Let's give credit where credit is seldom due ! . . . I shall miss Elma —I love her very much !

ERNEST. (*Anxiously.*) You haven't been telling her so, have you, Geoffrey ?

GEOFF. (*Starts.*) No—do you know, I never realised it until a few minutes ago—that's odd— because I realise now I love her very much—I suppose it's because I'm going to lose her !

ERNEST. Does she dislike me very much, Geoff ?

GEOFF. She loathes you, old friend !

ERNEST. You'll help me, Geoff—you'll tell her—

GEOFF. I'm sorry I didn't make a fuss of Elma—I love her very much !

ERNEST. You're irritating me, Geoffrey !

GEOFF. Good !

ERNEST. If I thought for a moment you had taken advantage of me during the time I thought I was in love with your wife, I——

GEOFF. I didn't—but I am exceedingly sorry I didn't—I love Elma very much ! I'm going to

miss her—I'm going to be very unhappy—indeed
I am !

ERNEST.   Look out !

(ELMA ENTERS.)

(BOTH *rise.*)

GEOFF.   Little Elma ! My dear little friend !

ELMA.   (*To* ERNEST.)   Why are you still here ?

GEOFF.   The game's up, Elma !

ELMA.   What do you mean ?   (*Sits R. of table.*)

GEOFF.   Nothing doing—it's off.   He's tumbled !

ELMA.   He hasn't !

GEOFF.   He has ! And it's a terrible thing for me
because it means that I'm going to lose you—
and I don't want to lose you because I love you
very much—indeed I do !

ELMA.   (*Rises.*)   Are you positive of that, Geoffrey?

GEOFF.   Absolutely !   I love you very much !

ERNEST.   Stop, Geoffrey ! How dare you speak
to my wife in that way ! Elma ! Please
listen to me—I'm terribly sorry, I don't know
what to say to you !

ELMA.   You're not asking me to forgive you and
take you back again ?

ERNEST.   Yes !—I know I have treated you
shamefully——

ELMA.   Nothing will induce me to ! (*Looks at*
ERNEST, *then at* GEOFFREY, *starts, speaks*

G

quietly.)   Besides, even if I wanted to—it's too late !

ERNEST.   What do you mean ?

ELMA.   (*Looks on the ground.*)   I have been unfaithful with him !

(GEOFFREY *starts*.)

ERNEST.   (*In anguish.*)   It isn't true !

ELMA.   It is !

ERNEST.   Geoffrey ! it's a lie, isn't it ?

GEOFF.   (*Hesitates—looks at door.*)   No, Ernest, old friend, it's the truth !

ERNEST.   (*Crosses and sinks into chair R.*)   My best friend—my best friend !

(ANNE *enters*.)

(GEOFFREY *and* ELMA *exchange glances.*)

ANNE.   Ernest, Ernest !   (*Looks at Ernest.*)   What does this mean—(*Shaking* ERNEST.)   What is the matter ?

GEOFF.   Be gentle with him, Anne—he's had some bad news !

ANNE.   (*Anxiously.*)   What ?

GEOFF.   He has discovered that his wife has been unfaithful with me !

[CURTAIN]

ACT III

SCENE : The same.

> (*They are all in exactly the same positions as they were when the Curtain fell on* ACT II.)

TIME : One second later.

> (*That there should be nothing left to chance, and that it should be perfectly clear to the audience that it is a second later,* ERNEST *should, in burying his face in his hands, have some distinctive coloured handkerchief in his hand.* GEOFFREY'S *hair is untidy—he is flushed and wears a perpetual smile.*)

ANNE. Ernest !

> (*He shakes his head.*)

Have you nothing to say to me.

ERNEST. Please, Sapphire—Anne !

ANNE. Ho ! This is too dreadful. Oh, stop smiling.

GEOFF. I won't—besides, I can't.

ANNE. (*Smells glass.*) I thought so ! (*To* ELMA.) You may have him, and I only hope that he won't bore you as he has me.

ELMA.   I think you are very kind.

(ERNEST *groans through all this*.)

GEOFF.   Ernest, when nature gave you the gift of
being able to make these curious noises, it was
her intention that you should not use them
publicly !

ANNE.   Ernest, please, I——

ERNEST.   No, no, I shall never lift my head again !

ELMA.   No one can say that is bad news !

(GEOFFREY *laughs*.)

ANNE.   (*To* GEOFFREY.)   When I leave this house
directly, my prayer is that I will be spared ever
seeing you again as long as I live !

GEOFF.   Let us pray that your prayer will be
favourably considered.

(ELMA *laughs*.)

ANNE.   I envy you your ability to laugh at
nothing !   But I am glad you can—(*looks at*
GEOFFREY) because you will have every opportunity offered you to in the future !   It is my
intention to leave for London this instant, that
I may see my lawyer to-night—do you understand what that means ?

GEOFF.   Perfectly !   And you may tell him I will
not defend—and the interview is to be charged
to Ernest !

ANNE. I am grateful to you, Mrs. Melton. I have wanted this opportunity for a long time !

(*Walks to door, bangs it after her.*)

ELMA. Noisy !

(*Pause—the front door bangs.*)

She's gone to her lawyer.

(ERNEST *lifts his head, looks at them both.*)

Ernest, you haven't kept your promise !

ERNEST. (*Shakes his head.*) My heart is broken !

GEOFF. That's a lie—the reason that you hid your face was because you were frightened that Anne would smack it—and after the cruel way you have treated her, you should have let her !

ERNEST. Be quiet !

GEOFF. I won't.

ERNEST. Tell me it isn't true, Elma—tell me you said those dreadful things to make me unhappy —to punish me—tell me it's a lie.

ELMA. I cannot tell a lie, Ernest !

GEOFF. Oh, I like that ! That's funny !

ERNEST. One more word from you, Lymes, and I'll throw you through that window.

GEOFF. Melton ! I must ask you to remember that you are a guest in this house.

ERNEST. You can't love this man, Elma—you can't !

ELMA. How could I have done what I have done if I don't, Ernest ?

ERNEST. No, no, you can't—I don't believe it !

GEOFF. Ernest, old friend—look at me very carefully.

ERNEST. Well ?

GEOFF. Now can't you see why she loves me ?

ERNEST. I can see every reason why she shouldn't !

GEOFF. I hate men who can't drink like gentlemen !

ERNEST. If it were any one else but this dreadful man ! Look at him.

ELMA. I don't know—after all, you did leave me alone with him for weeks for a not too attractive woman !

ERNEST. I know—I know—(*Appealing.*) Elma, I know I have behaved abominably, but if you will let me, and this man will leave us, I can explain !

ELMA. Ernest, that you could have preferred Sapphire to me, you never can explain !

GEOFF. Never !

ERNEST. I know, but——

ELMA. And it's too late ! It may be propinquity ! It may be that having lived with a gentleman for six years one imagines qualities in a playwright that do not exist, but as far as it is humanly possible for a woman to know her

own mind, I believe I love him. I believe I
love him very much ! But there is no obligation on your part, Geoffrey—there is no
reason why you should like me !

GEOFF. But I do ! I realize I like you enormously
—I can't tell you how much—and if this man
would leave us for a moment, I——

ELMA. Later !

ERNEST. Elma, for God's sake—is there nothing
I can do ?

ELMA. Nothing, Ernest, except do for me what
Sapphire is going to begin doing to-night for him,
give me my freedom.

ERNEST. If I tell you that I am prepared to overlook——

ELMA. I don't want you to overlook anything—
I want you to act on the information I have
given you and go to London and see your lawyer
to-night ! That is your wish, Geoffrey ?

GEOFF. Absolutely ! I insist !

ERNEST. Very well ! Very well !

ELMA. Thank you ! You're certain you want to
go on, Geoffrey ?

GEOFF. I have never been more certain of anything ! It's difficult to tell you how much I
like you in front of a third person—but——

ELMA. There will be difficulties—unpleasantness !

GEOFF. What do I care !

ELMA.   You're positive you like me enough to do this ?

GEOFF.   I have never been so positive of anything.

ELMA.   I'm glad ! I suppose for the moment I had better go home to my mother ?

GEOFF.   Certainly not ! You will have your things packed and we will go together to-night !

ELMA.   I would prefer that. Ernest ! Shall I see you before you go to your lawyer ?

(ERNEST *shakes his head.*)

(ELMA *exits.*)

ERNEST.   I could kill you, Lymes ?

GEOFF.   I didn't quite catch what you said, old friend ?

ERNEST.   I say I could kill you !

GEOFF.   Well, do speak up, there's a dear feller !

ERNEST.   That you could have done such a thing to me !

GEOFF.   Well, you did it to me for three weeks, and I didn't go about saying I wanted to kill you !

ERNEST.   What did I do to you ? I talked art, museums, Rome, literature, music, and all the other things your wife knows nothing about— is that immorality ?

GEOFF.   Of the worst kind.

ERNEST. You traitor!

GEOFF. I am not a traitor! I'm just an attractive feller who wins women without a word! I'm glad I didn't know my power over women before—it might have been very troublesome!

ERNEST. Stop smiling at nothing, you stupid ass! That you could have ever allowed my wife to be unfaithful with you is something I can't believe.

GEOFF. Oh! one moment! In self-defence—not a word again Elma, mind you—but there she grossly exaggerated.

ERNEST. What do you mean?

GEOFF. What I say! That she loves me there is no doubt whatever, but the infidelity she suggested was a gross exaggeration.

ERNEST. Are you telling me that Elma told me a lie?

GEOFF. It would be wrong of me to suggest that a woman I have just become engaged to could tell a lie—I only say she exaggerated!

ERNEST. I don't believe you!

GEOFF. Melton! Are you suggesting that if your wife had been unfaithful with me I would be such a cad as not to remember it?

ERNEST. Then why did she say it?

GEOFF. Ah! that's obvious. A determination

to leave nothing unsaid that would make it possible for her to ever have to be alone with you again! You bore her terribly, old friend!

ERNEST. One moment! If she lied when she told me that, perhaps she lied when she said she loved you!

GEOFF. No, Melton, that is one of the few occasions when she will have ever told either of us the truth!

ERNEST. You conceited ass!

GEOFF. I'm sorry you say that; all my life I have tried in the hour of triumph to bear myself like all great men with artificial modesty!

ERNEST. Great men! Last night I picked up one of your plays, I read the first act—with the second I broke a window! You'll be known to posterity as a man who had the good fortune to live in an age when Managers couldn't read!

GEOFF. Oh, what a mean way of attacking the Jews!

(ELMA *enters from garden. She stands by the curtains of the door listening, unknown to them.*)

ERNEST. Geoff, I'm sorry I said that—for God's sake—you don't love her, do you?

GEOFF. I certainly do—I didn't realise how much until I was going to lose her—all the time you left me alone with her I realise now, apart from the fact that it was helping me to lose Anne, I liked being with her! I liked it very much! Without knowing it, I was in love with her all the time!

ERNEST. Ho! Ho!

GEOFF. It's no good going on with those noises; nothing would induce her to go back to you!

ERNEST. If you sent her she would!

GEOFF. She wouldn't; and why should I? I adore the girl! She's attractive, amusing, a grand companion, and everything I like in a woman!

ERNEST. And another man's wife!

GEOFF. If you allowed yourself the privilege of forgetting it, surely I may?

ERNEST. If you really loved her you wouldn't drag her through this scandal!

GEOFF. What scandal! And supposing there is, what do she and I care about scandal? Melton, you're an impertinent feller! You leave your wife alone with me for weeks, you allow us to discover we have much in common—grow to like each other—and when you are bored with my wife you calmly say, ' Give me back my own!' You're an impertinent feller, Melton!

ERNEST. I love her!

GEOFF. So do I! And she loves me! And I

am confident we could make each other very happy ! I have no doubt our married life will be a great and permanent success ! And let me tell you something else, I'm putting a woman in Percy's cage, because I realise now canaries cannot sing by seed alone. Anyway, I know I can't.

(ELMA, *unknown to him, blows him a kiss.*)

ERNEST.   Won't you give her back to me ?

GEOFF.   No, I won't !

ERNEST.   Very well, then ! I shall divorce her at once !

GEOFF.   Good !

ERNEST.   And I know it isn't done—but I will do it—I will ask for the heaviest damages I can get ! And settle them on her !

GEOFF.   That 's funny.   The Court will award you a lot when I tell them what you did.

ERNEST.   And give your own wife away——

(*Pause.*)

that would be a charming thing to do, wouldn't it ? But I'm sure you're capable of it.

GEOFF.   Do what you like !

ERNEST.   Pretty reading it will make. Large head-lines : ' Playwright runs away with greatest friend's wife.'—in larger head-lines :

' Judge gives playwright severe dressing down '——

GEOFF. All his business is—to pronounce the decree !

ERNEST. Very likely—but judges like their bit of fun like other people ! Oh, a nice booing you will get on the next first night you have.

GEOFF. Who cares whether they boo or not ?

ERNEST. You do, or you wouldn't have gone white ?

GEOFF. I haven't ! The brandy's worn off and I've become normal again !

ERNEST. And what a pretty reception you'll receive from your club friends the first time you go in after having run away with your best friend's wife !

GEOFF. They'd have a damn nerve to criticise anybody else's moral life !

ERNEST. In self-protection *they'd* have to—they don't want to be found out ! There are too many unhappily married men committed to marriage for life—too many men frightened they might lose their wives for them to let you get away with mine, scot-free ! Those men will make your life hell, Lymes !

GEOFF. Pooh ! What do I care ?

ERNEST. Anyway, it would do one thing for you, it would save you ever having to bother again when the Honours list comes out—you'll know that you are still *Mr.* Lymes.

GEOFF. Pooh! What playwright ever wanted to be a knight?

ERNEST. None—until they are offered it! And then they accept, it like the lawyers, for their wives' sake. Every time you enter a public room, you'll never know whether they are saying, 'That is Lymes, the playwright,' or 'Lymes, the home-wrecker'—you'll never know peace of mind again, Lymes—it may interfere with your work—it may even mean you will never write another play!

GEOFF. You're talking nonsense!

ERNEST. You know I am not! It takes the most enormous courage to do what you're doing, and only one man and a woman in thousands has the courage to do it! It's public opinion that keeps men and women together in this world! It's a much stronger bond than love!

GEOFF. What do I care for public opinion?

ERNEST. Then there's no point in my staying any longer—I'll do what Elma asks of me!

GEOFF. One moment!

ERNEST. Well?

GEOFF. Come back here and sit down!

(ERNEST *sits down*.)

Understand this, Melton—if I were alone in this I wouldn't hesitate—but I have to think of Elma. Do you understand that?

ERNEST. I'm glad to hear it!

GEOFF. And if I appear to be weakening, it is solely on her account—remember this, I like her too much to do anything that would make her unhappy! And from what you have described to me, I must ask myself, ' would she be happy? '

ERNEST. If you did such a dishonourable thing, how could she be happy?

GEOFF. Am I to understand that there is anything dishonourable in taking an unhappy woman from a dull man?

ERNEST. Nothing! But acknowledge it and you'll have to find hotel accommodation for ninety per cent. of the married women of England.

GEOFF. That's true! That's terribly true! Melton! I shall have to seriously reconsider my views of men who look as stupid as you do!

ERNEST. Why?

GEOFF. Because from this conversation I have gathered that underneath that incredible face and moustache there's brains!

ERNEST. I am always being mistaken for a Conservative!

GEOFF. Belonging as you do to an old and

aristocratic family I wonder you don't write articles for the papers !

ERNEST.   I can't write.

GEOFF.   Many other members of the aristocracy have not been discouraged by that inability, Melton ! (*Rises.*) But you have made me realise the gravity of what I was threatening to do—I must forget myself and think only of Elma !

ERNEST.   I should think of myself, too—if I were you—it's you who will cop it worst.

GEOFF.   What do I care what they say of me ? Leave me out of it and think only of Elma !

ERNEST.   Very well !

GEOFF.   If I do the right thing and take her from you, I ruin her—if I don't, I make her terribly unhappy ! I am in the unenviable position of either the public thinking me a cad —or your wife being sure that I am !

ERNEST.   That's the position.

GEOFF.   Do you dull men walking up the aisle of a church ever realise the responsibilities you are about to thrust upon some other unsuspecting man ?

ERNEST.   No !

GEOFF.   Exactly ! I am disturbed. What is the solution to this story ? The obvious end is heroism and self-sacrifice on my part. Melton, painful as it is, I give you back your wife !

ERNEST. And rightly.

GEOFF. One moment! Will Elma agree to take you back!—I'd forgotten that!

ERNEST. Naturally, at first she will make a scene, but——

GEOFF. Scene? I cannot bear scenes with women, Melton!

ERNEST. I sympathize! But you'll have many if you marry her—and only one if you don't!

GEOFF. Odd you should look so stupid! Shall we run it as it were on the lines of honour?

ERNEST. Not much good with Elma! She's very likely listening at the door the whole time!

GEOFF. What do you say.

(ELMA *slips behind the curtain*.)

Ssh. I won't be a moment, Ernest! (*Goes to door—opens it*.) You have no right to make suggestions of that kind against your wife. And I would be glad if you did not add to my already considerable nervous condition, Melton?

(ELMA *steps out*.)

ERNEST. You have nothing to be nervous about, Geoff—after all, you are only doing a very honourable thing in returning a woman to her husband!

H

GEOFF.   Women hate having honourable things
done to them! There's going to be a scene,
Melton! and I hate scenes with women! I
think it would be better if I wrote to her.

ERNEST.   Wouldn't that be cowardly, Geoff!
You couldn't do that—you must face her!

GEOFF.   Melton! I will either write to your wife,
or run away with her! My sensitive nature
forbids me to argue with her!

ERNEST.   Forget you are a writer and be a man,
Geoff.   Listen! There are far greater things in
the world than love! To break asunder those
who have been joined together. It is not for you
to have the unhappy married people of the world
pointing the finger of envy at the one you love—
and all the similar platitudes that men have been
telling women for years!

GEOFF.   Melton! I will write all that to her.

(ELMA *leaves the curtain.*)

ERNEST.   She'll follow you—you'll have to have
the scene! And you could do it so convincingly!

GEOFF.   I doubt it very much.

ERNEST.   I'm certain you could.

GEOFF.   You really think I could?

ERNEST.   I shall be very surprised if I don't find
myself crying bitterly! If you can only get

going, it ought to be very beautiful. You have such an amazing personality, Geoff !

GEOFF. Fetch her ! One moment ! in the event of my being able to persuade Elma to take you back, what is my position with Anne ? Ah ! That has to be considered.

ERNEST. After the things she has said to you, she couldn't possibly expect you to take her back !

GEOFF. You're sure ? Because if——

ERNEST. Of course ! How could she ! You're as free as the air.

GEOFF. Fetch her. (*Makes movement towards door.*)

(ELMA *enters.*)

(GEOFFREY *and* ERNEST *look at each other anxiously.*)

ELMA. (*To* ERNEST.) Still here, Ernest ? I thought you promised to go to your lawyer at once ?

ERNEST. I know ! But——

GEOFF. After you left us, Elma, he had what might be called a manly attack of hysteria— and I had no option but to let him stay !

ELMA. I've packed, Geoffrey—and I find there's a train we can catch at seven o'clock !

GEOFF. Yes—yes—we will catch it. Ernest, be a good feller and ask Morton to pack for me !

ELMA.   He has !   Your things are with mine in the hall !

GEOFF.   Good !   Ernest, old chap, tell Morton to order us a taxi.

ELMA.   I have already asked him to do that, too !

GEOFF.   Good.

ELMA.   Does this obvious endeavour to get rid of the good feller—and good chap—mean you wish to speak to me alone ?

GEOFF.   Good heavens, no !   What makes you think that ?

ELMA.   I thought perhaps Rasputin had been busy during my absence !

GEOFF.   Ras—— Ernest has said only the most charming and attractive things about you, Elma !

ELMA.   Really !

GEOFF.   If your life with me would be happy he is not only willing but anxious to give you your freedom at once !

ELMA.   Why doesn't he do it ?

GEOFF.   His one thought is for you—he has none for himself.

ELMA.   How nice.

GEOFF.   His unselfish love for you has touched me very deeply—I never thought Ernest capable of such fine affection !

ELMA. I am a little bewildered—are you running away with me or Ernest ?

GEOFF. Elma ! please ! this is a very sacred moment.

ELMA. Sorry ! But I thought if you were trying to get out yourself—it was a pity to waste all these words—as you only have to say so.

GEOFF. Elma ! As long as I live—with you— or without you—you will always be the most divine woman I have ever known !

ELMA. Then what are we waiting for ?

GEOFF. Because before you take this plunge into the abyss of—of—I think it my duty to warn you of the grave step you are taking.

ELMA. Geoffrey, you've only got to say—' Elma, I made a mistake—I haven't the courage—I am not big enough to face the criticism of the world '—and I shall be very understanding ! I shall be very sympathetic.

GEOFF. I ? I ? What do I care for criticism ? Good God ! How curious women are ! Here am I offering to make the greatest sacrifice I have ever made—and you suggest that I am thinking of myself ! It's you I am thinking of. Supposing in the years to come—you realise there are far greater things in the world than love——

ELMA. —Or had one the right to break the promise to the Vicar——

GEOFF. Yes.

ELMA. —Or is it a good example to those who follow us.

GEOFF. Yes, if you like !

ELMA. In brief—before I take this serious step, you feel I should consider all these things—do you suggest I should also consider returning to Ernest ?

GEOFF. I realise to leave a man whom I now recognize as one who loves you very deeply—I am right, Ernest, in saying that ? ——

ERNEST. Yes, Geoffrey.

GEOFF. —For ever to have it on your conscience his lasting misery is due to you—I sincerely say we should both consider it very seriously.

ELMA. Your view being it is wrong to accept any happiness at the cost of others—it is better to be miserable oneself than make another.

GEOFF. I say, conscious of the sorrow it will cause me, we should pause before doing anything so serious.

ELMA. Most touching. I had no idea you had such a beautiful nature, Geoffrey. Do you know why you are a second-class playwright ?

GEOFF. What do you mean ?

ELMA. Because you are a second-class man. A plumber with a gift of dialogue. You neither have nor ever could furnish the world with an idea—you haven't the courage to have one.

You would sacrifice the greatest happiness in the world rather than be criticised by the man who lives next door—even though you don't know him. In your little life of egoism you never pass a church without hoping and wondering if there will be a lot of people at your memorial service. Your only idea of love is to take a little flat and hide the little lady in it. To possess the good opinion of all men you even cheat yourself —a man without an idea—a man without courage. (*To* ERNEST.) With all your faults you are a better man than your little friend.

ERNEST. I think so.

GEOFF. I protest. What I have suggested is purely out of consideration for you.

ELMA. If you believed your wife was still in this house and not on her way to her lawyer's, would you have made these suggestions?

GEOFF. Yes, I should.

ELMA. If it were proved to you—not loving her— that she cares for you as much as Ernest cares for me—would you sacrifice yourself and take her back? Why don't you answer?

GEOFF. If Anne cares for me as much as Ernest cares for you—I should.

ELMA. She does. Fetch her, Ernest—she is sitting in the hall, crying.

GEOFF.   One moment !

ELMA.   Fetch her, Ernest !

(ERNEST *goes out*.)

GEOFF.   What does this mean ?

ELMA.   It means that I gathered from those tears that within a few minutes of your wife leaving this house for ever—she who was contemptuous of everything normal—anything ordinary, realised that, after all, she was as conventionally-minded as you are. She discovered for the first time what being respectably married meant to her—she discovered it might be infinitely easier to live with a man you despise than face the smile of public opinion—in a flash she discovered what a silly thing she was doing—and having discovered how stupid it would be to live on only a little of your income instead of nearly all of it—she decided to return and tell you that she loved you.

GEOFF.   But—but——

(ERNEST *and* ANNE *enter*.)

ANNE.   You want me, Geoffrey.

ELMA.   Am I right in saying that you suddenly discovered within a few minutes of leaving your home for ever, your feelings as regards that home and your husband underwent a serious change—you suddenly discovered how deep your affection was for both of them ?

ANNE. Yes.

ELMA. And I am happy to tell you Geoffrey feels the same—he feels that there are far greater things in the world than love—to break asunder those who have been joined together—and the many other platitudes all men discover when they don't wish to do a thing. In effect, Geoffrey has told me there is no other happiness in life for me other than with my husband— consequently there can be none for him other than with his wife—so, feeling as he does, I ask you to forgive him and take him back.

ANNE. Very well.

ELMA. I'm glad. (*Moving towards door.*) So there's only one thing left for me to do—and that is to wish you all good-bye.

(ERNEST *rises.*)

Why do you move, Ernest ?

ERNEST. I'm going with you, aren't I ?

ELMA. Don't be absurd. I'm not as good, perhaps, as Geoffrey and Mrs. Lymes—but I have courage, Ernest—I could no more think of going back to that awful life I have known with you, than fly.

ERNEST. Where—where—are you going?

ELMA. I?   I'm going to find another co-respondent.

(ELMA exits.)

[CURTAIN]

PRINTED IN GREAT BRITAIN BY
WYMAN AND SONS, LIMITED
LONDON, FAKENHAM AND READING

OTHER POPULAR PLAYS

George Pleydell Bancroft—

THE WARE CASE

A PLAY IN FOUR ACTS. *Second Edition.*
Fcap. 8vo. 3s. 6d. net.

P. G. Wodehouse—

GOOD-MORNING, BILL!

A THREE-ACT COMEDY. With stage directions
by the author. (Based on the Hungarian of
LADISLAUS FODOR.) *Crown 8vo. 3s. 6d. net.*

A play full of fun and frolic. With the stage directions added
it becomes more than a play—a comic history.

Paul Raynal—

THE UNKNOWN WARRIOR

A TRAGEDY IN THREE ACTS. The English
Version by CECIL LEWIS. *Large Crown 8vo.*
7s. 6d. net.

This play crystallises, in scenes of great beauty and dramatic
power, all that thinking people have ever associated with the
horror of war, the nobility of the men who wage it, and the tragedy
of the women who watch it.

Edward Knoblock —

KISMET

AN ARABIAN NIGHT IN THREE ACTS. *Fifth*
Edition. Fcap. 8vo. Paper Covers. 2s. net.

Kismet is a play that strives to capture, not only the imagination and the adventure, but also the colour of the East.

J. E. Harold Terry—

GENERAL POST

Second Edition. Fcap. 8vo. 3s. 6d. net.

This book is a very successful and amusing play.

E. V. Lucas—

THE SAME STAR

A COMEDY IN THREE ACTS. *Fcap. 8vo.*
3s. 6d. net.

With this book Mr. Lucas makes his bow as a dramatist. It
is a comedy of the course of true love above stairs and below.

METHUEN'S GENERAL LITERATURE

A SELECTION OF
MESSRS. METHUEN'S
PUBLICATIONS

This Catalogue contains only a selection of the more important books published by Messrs. Methuen. A complete catalogue of their publications may be obtained on application.

ALLEN (J. W.).
A HISTORY OF POLITICAL THOUGHT IN THE SIXTEENTH CENTURY. £1 1s. net.

ARMSTRONG (Anthony).
WARRIORS AT EASE. WARRIORS STILL AT EASE. PERCIVAL AND I. HOW TO DO IT. Each 3s. 6d. net.

BAIN (F. W.).
IN THE GREAT GOD'S HAIR. A DRAUGHT OF THE BLUE. AN INCARNATION OF THE SNOW. A MINE OF FAULTS. A DIGIT OF THE MOON. THE LIVERY OF EVE. A HEIFER OF THE DAWN. AN ESSENCE OF THE DUSK. THE DESCENT OF THE SUN. THE ASHES OF A GOD. BUBBLES OF THE FOAM. A SYRUP OF THE BEES. THE SUBSTANCE OF A DREAM. 5s. net each. AN ECHO OF THE SPHERES. 10s. 6d. net.

BATESON (William).
LETTERS FROM THE STEPPE. Illustrated. 7s. 6d. net.

BELLOC (H.).
A HISTORY OF ENGLAND. In 5 vols. Vols. I, II and III. Each, 15s. net. MARIE ANTOINETTE. Illustrated. Demy 8vo, 18s. net. PARIS. THE PYRENEES. Each, Illustrated, Crown 8vo, 8s. 6d. net. ON NOTHING. HILLS AND THE SEA. ON SOMETHING. FIRST AND LAST. THIS AND THAT AND THE OTHER. ON. ON EVERYTHING. ON ANYTHING. EMMANUEL BURDEN. Each, 3s. 6d. net. HILLS AND THE SEA. Illustrated in Colour by DONALD MAXWELL. 15s. net.

BIRMINGHAM (George A.).
A WAYFARER IN HUNGARY. Illustrated, 8s. 6d. net. SPILLIKINS. SHIPS AND SEALING-WAX. Two Books of Essays. Each 3s. 6d. net.

CHESTERTON (G. K.).
GENERALLY SPEAKING. 6s. net. THE OUTLINE OF SANITY. ALL THINGS CONSIDERED. TREMENDOUS TRIFLES. FANCIES VERSUS FADS. CHARLES DICKENS. THE BALLAD OF THE WHITE HORSE. ALARMS AND DISCURSIONS. A MISCELLANY OF MEN. THE USES OF DIVERSITY. Each 3s. 6d. net. A GLEAMING COHORT. 2s. 6d. net. WINE, WATER, AND SONG. 1s. 6d. net. THE BALLAD OF THE WHITE HORSE Illustrated by Robert Austin. 12s. 6d. net.

DICKINSON (G. Lowes).

THE GREEK VIEW OF LIFE. *Fifteenth Edition.* 5s. net.

DOLLS' HOUSE (THE QUEEN'S).

THE BOOK OF THE QUEEN'S DOLLS' HOUSE. Vol. I. THE HOUSE, Edited by A. C. BENSON, C.V.O., and SIR LAWRENCE WEAVER, K.B.E. Vol. II. THE LIBRARY. Edited by E. V. LUCAS. Illustrated. £6 6s. net.

EINSTEIN (Albert).

RELATIVITY: THE SPECIAL AND THE GENERAL THEORY. *Seventh Edition.* 5s. net. SIDELIGHTS ON RELATIVITY. 3s. 6d. net. THE MEANING OF RELATIVITY. 5s. net. THE BROWNIAN MOVEMENT. 5s. net.

ERMAN (A.).

THE LITERATURE OF THE ANCIENT EGYPTIANS: Poems, Narratives, and Manuals of Instruction from the Third and Second Millennia B.C. Translated by Dr. A. M. BLACKMAN. £1 1s. net.

FYLEMAN (Rose).

FAIRIES AND CHIMNEYS. *Twenty-first Edition.* THE FAIRY GREEN. *Tenth Edition.* THE FAIRY FLUTE. *Tenth Edition.* THE RAINBOW CAT AND OTHER STORIES. *Second Edition.* FORTY GOOD-NIGHT TALES. *Eighth Edition.* EIGHT LITTLE PLAYS FOR CHILDREN. *Third Edition.* FAIRIES AND FRIENDS. *Second Edition.* THE ADVENTURE CLUB. Illustrated. FORTY GOOD-MORNING TALES. *Third Edition.* SEVEN LITTLE PLAYS FOR CHILDREN. Each 3s. 6d. net. A SMALL CRUSE. 4s. 6d. net. THE ROSE FYLEMAN FAIRY BOOK. Illustrated. 10s. 6d. net. A GARLAND OF ROSE'S: COLLECTED POEMS. Illustrated. 10s. 6d. net. OLD-FASHIONED GIRLS. Illustrated. 7s. 6d. net. LETTY: A STUDY OF A CHILD. Illustrated. 6s. net. A PRINCESS COMES TO OUR TOWN. Illustrated. 5s. net. A LITTLE CHRISTMAS BOOK. Illustrated. 2s. net.

GIBBON (Edward).

THE DECLINE AND FALL OF THE ROMAN EMPIRE. Edited, with Notes, Appendixes, and Maps, by J. B. BURY. Illustrated. Seven Volumes. Each 15s. net. Also, unillustrated. Seven Volumes. Each 7s. 6d. net.

GLOVER (T. R.).

THE CONFLICT OF RELIGIONS IN THE EARLY ROMAN EMPIRE. POETS AND PURITANS. VIRGIL. Each 10s. 6d. net. FROM PERICLES TO PHILIP. 12s. 6d. net.

GRAHAM (Harry).

THE WORLD WE LAUGH IN: MORE DEPORTMENTAL DITTIES. Illustrated by "FISH." *Eighth Edition.* 5s. net. STRAINED RELATIONS. Illustrated by H. STUART MENZIES and HENDY. 6s. net. THE WORLD'S WORKERS. Illustrated by "FOUGASSE." 5s. net.

GRAHAME (Kenneth).

THE WIND IN THE WILLOWS. *Nineteenth Edition.* 7s. 6d. net. Also Pocket Edition, 3s. 6d. net. Also illustrated by WYNDHAM PAYNE. 7s. 6d. net.

HADFIELD (J. A.).

PSYCHOLOGY AND MORALS. *Seventh Edition.* 6s. net.

HALL (H. R.).

THE ANCIENT HISTORY OF THE NEAR EAST. Illustrated. *Seventh*

Edition, Revised. £1 1s. net. THE CIVILIZATION OF GREECE IN THE BRONZE AGE. Illustrated. £1 10s. net.

HERBERT (A. P.).

HONEYBUBBLE & CO. 6s. net. MISLEADING CASES IN THE COMMON LAW. Introduction by LORD HEWART. 5s. net. THE BOMBER GIPSY. 3s. 6d. net. "LIGHT ARTICLES ONLY." Illustrated. 6s. net. THE WHEREFORE AND THE WHY. "TINKER, TAILOR . . ." Each Illustrated. 3s. 6d. net. THE SECRET BATTLE. 3s. 6d. net.

HOLDSWORTH (W. S.).

A HISTORY OF ENGLISH LAW. Nine Volumes. Each £1 5s. net.

HUTTON (Edward).

CITIES OF SICILY. Illustrated. 10s. 6d. net. MILAN AND LOMBARDY. THE CITIES OF ROMAGNA AND THE MARCHES. SIENA AND SOUTHERN TUSCANY. THE CITIES OF SPAIN. NAPLES AND SOUTHERN ITALY. Each, illustrated, 8s. 6d. net. VENICE AND VENETIA. A WAYFARER IN UNKNOWN TUSCANY. THE CITIES OF UMBRIA. COUNTRY WALKS ABOUT FLORENCE. ROME. FLORENCE AND NORTHERN TUSCANY. Each, illustrated, 7s. 6d. net.

INGE (W. R.), C.V.O., D.D., Dean of St. Paul's.

CHRISTIAN MYSTICISM. (The Bampton Lectures of 1899.) *Sixth Edition.* 7s. 6d. net.

KIPLING (Rudyard).

BARRACK-ROOM BALLADS. *246th Thousand.* THE SEVEN SEAS. *180th Thousand.* THE FIVE NATIONS. *143rd Thousand.* DEPARTMENTAL DITTIES. *116th Thousand.* THE YEARS BETWEEN. *95th Thousand.* Four editions of these famous volumes of poems are now published, viz. :—Crown 8vo, Buckram, 7s. 6d. net ; Fcap. 8vo, Cloth, 6s. net ; Leather, 7s. 6d. net ; and *Service Edition.* Two Vols. each book. Square Fcap. 8vo, 3s. 6d. net each Vol. A KIPLING ANTHOLOGY— VERSE. *Third Edition.* Cloth, 6s. net and 3s. 6d. net ; Leather, 7s. 6d. net. TWENTY POEMS. *464th Thousand.* 1s. net. A CHOICE OF SONGS. *Second Edition.* 2s. net.

KNOX (E. V.) ("Evoe").

WONDERFUL OUTINGS. PARODIES REGAINED. Each 5s. net. THESE LIBERTIES. 4s. 6d. net. FICTION AS SHE IS WROTE. FANCY NOW ! QUAINT SPECIMENS. HERE'S MISERY ! Each 6s. net. AWFUL OCCASIONS. GORGEOUS TIMES. IT OCCURS TO ME. Each 3s. 6d. net.

LAMB (Charles and Mary).

THE COMPLETE WORKS. Edited by E. V. LUCAS. A New and Revised Edition in six volumes. With Frontispieces. Each 6s. net. The Volumes are :—1, MISCELLANEOUS PROSE. 2, ELIA AND THE LAST ESSAYS OF ELIA. 3, BOOKS FOR CHILDREN. 4, PLAYS AND POEMS. 5 and 6, LETTERS.

SELECTED LETTERS. Chosen and Edited by G. T. CLAPTON. 3s. 6d. net. THE CHARLES LAMB DAY BOOK. Compiled by E. V. LUCAS. 6s. net.

LANKESTER (Sir Ray).

SCIENCE FROM AN EASY CHAIR. First Series. SCIENCE FROM AN EASY CHAIR. Second Series. DIVERSIONS OF A NATURALIST. GREAT AND SMALL THINGS. Each illustrated. 7s. 6d. net. SECRETS OF EARTH AND SEA. Illustrated. 8s. 6d. net.

LODGE (Sir Oliver).

MAN AND THE UNIVERSE, 7s. 6d. net and 3s. 6d. net. THE SURVIVAL OF MAN, 7s. 6d. net. REASON AND BELIEF, 2s. net. THE SUBSTANCE OF FAITH, 2s. net. MODERN PROBLEMS, 3s. 6d. net. RAYMOND, 10s. 6d. net. RAYMOND REVISED, 6s. net. RELATIVITY, 1s. net.

LUCAS (E. V.).

THE LIFE OF CHARLES LAMB. 2 Vols. £1 1s. net. EDWIN AUSTIN ABBEY, R.A. 2 Vols. £6 6s. net. THE COLVINS AND THEIR FRIENDS, £1 1s. net. A WANDERER IN ROME. A WANDERER IN HOLLAND. A WANDERER IN LONDON. LONDON REVISITED (REVISED). A WANDERER IN PARIS. A WANDERER IN FLORENCE. A WANDERER IN VENICE. Each 10s. 6d. net. A WANDERER AMONG PICTURES. 8s. 6d. net. E. V. LUCAS'S LONDON. £1 net. INTRODUCING LONDON. INTRODUCING PARIS. Each, 2s. 6d. net. THE OPEN ROAD. 6s. net. Also, illustrated by CLAUDE A. SHEPPERSON. 10s. 6d. net. Also, India Paper. Leather, 7s. 6d. net. THE JOY OF LIFE. Cloth. 6s. net. Leather. 7s. 6d net. Also India Paper. Leather, 7s. 6d. net. THE FRIENDLY TOWN. FIRESIDE AND SUNSHINE. CHARACTER AND COMEDY. Each 6s. net. THE GENTLEST ART. 6s. 6d. net. THE SECOND POST. 6s. net. THE GENTLEST ART AND THE SECOND POST. (1 vol.) 7s. 6d. net. HER INFINITE VARIETY. GOOD COMPANY. ONE DAY AND ANOTHER. OLD LAMPS FOR NEW. LOITERER'S HARVEST. CLOUD AND SILVER. A BOSWELL OF BAGHDAD. 'TWIXT EAGLE AND DOVE. THE PHANTOM JOURNAL. GIVING AND RECEIVING. LUCK OF THE YEAR. ENCOUNTERS AND DIVERSIONS. ZIGZAGS IN FRANCE. EVENTS AND EMBROIDERIES. 365 DAYS AND ONE MORE. A FRONDED ISLE. A ROVER I WOULD BE. Each 6s. net. URBANITIES. Illustrated by G. L. STAMPA. 5s. net. "THE MORE I SEE OF MEN . . .". OUT OF A CLEAR SKY. Each 3s. 6d. net. *MR. PUNCH'S* COUNTY SONGS. Illustrated by E. H. SHEPARD. 10s. 6d. net. YOU KNOW WHAT PEOPLE ARE. Illustrated by GEORGE MORROW. 5s. net. PLAYTIME & COMPANY. Illustrated by E. H. SHEPARD. 7s. 6d. net. THE SAME STAR: A Comedy in Three Acts. 3s. 6d. net. LITTLE BOOKS ON GREAT MASTERS. Each 5s. net. ROVING EAST AND ROVING WEST. 5s. net. See also DOLLS' HOUSE (THE QUEEN'S) and LAMB (CHARLES and MARY).

LUCAS (E. V.) and FINCK (Herman).

Twelve Songs from " Playtime & Company." Words by E. V. Lucas. Music by Herman Finck. 7s. 6d. net.

LYND (Robert).

THE BLUE LION. THE PEAL OF BELLS. THE MONEY-BOX. THE ORANGE TREE. THE LITTLE ANGEL. Each Fcap. 8vo, 3s. 6d. net. THE GOLDFISH. THE PLEASURES OF IGNORANCE. OLD FRIENDS IN FICTION. THE GREEN MAN. Each 5s. net.

McDOUGALL (William).

AN INTRODUCTION TO SOCIAL PSYCHOLOGY (*Twenty-first Edition*), 10s. 6d. net ; BODY AND MIND (*Seventh Edition*), 12s. 6d. net ; AN OUTLINE OF PSYCHOLOGY (*Fourth Edition*), 10s. 6d. net ; NATIONAL WELFARE AND NATIONAL DECAY, 6s. net. ETHICS AND SOME MODERN WORLD PROBLEMS (*Second Edition*), 7s. 6d. net. AN OUTLINE OF ABNORMAL PSYCHOLOGY. 15s. net. CHARACTER AND THE CONDUCT OF LIFE. (*Third Edition*), 10s. 6d. net. PSYCHOLOGY AND MODERN MATERIALISM. 7s. 6d. net.

MAETERLINCK (Maurice).

THE BLUE BIRD. 6s. net and 2s. 6d. net. Also, illustrated by F. CAYLEY ROBINSON. 10s. 6d. net. THE BETROTHAL, 6s. net, paper 3s. 6d. net. DEATH, 3s. 6d. net. OUR ETERNITY, 6s. net. THE UNKNOWN GUEST, 6s. net. THE WRACK OF THE STORM, 6s. net. THE MIRACLE OF SAINT ANTHONY, 3s. 6d. net. THE BURGOMASTER OF STILEMONDE, 5s. net. MOUNTAIN PATHS, 6s. net. MARY MAGDALENE, 2s. net. TYLTYL, Told for Children (illustrated), 21s. net (All Translated by A. TEIXEIRA DE MATTOS). POEMS, 5s. net (Done into English by BERNARD MIALL). THE CLOUD THAT LIFTED AND THE POWER OF THE DEAD (Translated by F. M. ATKINSON), 7s. 6d. net. THE GREAT SECRET (Translated by BERNARD MIALL), 7s. 6d. net.

MALLET (Sir C. E.).

A HISTORY OF THE UNIVERSITY OF OXFORD. 3 Vols. Illustrated. Each £1 1s. net.

METHUEN (Sir A.).

AN ANTHOLOGY OF MODERN VERSE. 157th Thousand. SHAKESPEARE TO HARDY: An Anthology of English Lyrics. 19th Thousand. Each, Fcap. 8vo, Cloth, 6s. net; Leather, 7s. 6d. net.

MILNE (A. A.).

NOT THAT IT MATTERS. Eighth Edition. IF I MAY. Ninth Edition. THE DAY'S PLAY. Fourteenth Edition. THE HOLIDAY ROUND. Tenth Edition. ONCE A WEEK. Eleventh Edition. THE SUNNY SIDE. Ninth Edition. Each 3s. 6d. net. WHEN WE WERE VERY YOUNG. 179th Thousand. WINNIE-THE-POOH. 96th Thousand. NOW WE ARE SIX. 109th Thousand. THE HOUSE AT POOH CORNER. Each illustrated by E. H. SHEPARD. 7s. 6d. net. Leather, 10s. 6d. net. FOR THE LUNCHEON INTERVAL. Second Edition. 1s. 6d. net.

MILNE (A. A.) and FRASER-SIMSON (H.).

FOURTEEN SONGS FROM "WHEN WE WERE VERY YOUNG." (Twelfth Edition.) TEDDY BEAR AND OTHER SONGS (from the same). SONGS FROM "NOW WE ARE SIX." (Second Edition.) MORE "VERY YOUNG" SONGS. Each, Royal 4to, 7s. 6d. net. THE KING'S BREAKFAST. (Third Edition.) Music 4to, 3s. 6d. net.

MORTON (H. V.).

THE HEART OF LONDON. Fcap. 8vo, 3s. 6d. net. Also, Illustrated, 7s. 6d. net. THE SPELL OF LONDON. THE NIGHTS OF LONDON. Each Fcap. 8vo, 3s. 6d. net. THE LONDON YEAR. IN SEARCH OF ENGLAND. THE CALL OF ENGLAND. Each, Illustrated, 7s. 6d. net.

OMAN (Sir Charles).

A HISTORY OF THE ART OF WAR IN THE MIDDLE AGES, A.D. 378–1485. Second Edition, Revised and Enlarged. 2 Vols. Illustrated. Demy 8vo, £1 16s. net.

OXENHAM (John).

Eight Volumes of Poems. Small Pott 8vo, 1s. 3d. net each volume. BEES IN AMBER. (2s. net.) ALL'S WELL. THE KING'S HIGH WAY. THE VISION SPLENDID. THE FIERY CROSS. HEARTS COURAGEOUS. HIGH ALTARS. ALL CLEAR!

PETRIE (Sir Flinders).

A HISTORY OF EGYPT. Illustrated. Six Volumes. Crown 8vo. 1, FROM THE IST TO XVITH DYNASTY (12s. net). 2, THE XVIITH AND XVIIITH DYNASTIES (9s. net). 3, XIXTH TO XXXTH DYNASTIES (12s. net). 4, PTOLEMAIC EGYPT. EDWYN BEVAN. (15s. net.) 5, EGYPT UNDER

ROMAN RULE. J. G. MILNE. (12s. net.) 6, EGYPT IN THE MIDDLE AGES. STANLEY LANE-POOLE. (10s. net.)

PRIESTLEY (J. B.).
APES AND ANGELS. Fcap. 8vo, 5s. net.

RALEIGH (Sir Walter).
THE LETTERS OF SIR WALTER RALEIGH. Edited by LADY RALEIGH. 2 Vols. *Second Edition.* 18s. net. SELECTED LETTERS. 7s. 6d. net.

STEVENSON (R. L.).
LETTERS TO HIS FAMILY AND FRIENDS. Selected and Edited by SIR SIDNEY COLVIN. Four Volumes. *Fifth Edition.* Fcap. 8vo, 6s. net each. VAILIMA LETTERS. 7s. 6d. net. Also, 3s. 6d. net.

THOMAS (Sir William Beach), K.B.E.
THE STORY OF "THE SPECTATOR", 1828–1928. Illustrated. 10s. 6d. net.

TILDEN (William T.).
THE ART OF LAWN TENNIS. SINGLES AND DOUBLES. THE TENNIS RACKET. Each illustrated. 6s. net. LAWN TENNIS FOR YOUNG PLAYERS. LAWN TENNIS FOR CLUB PLAYERS. LAWN TENNIS FOR MATCH PLAYERS. Each illustrated. 2s. 6d. net. THE COMMON SENSE OF LAWN TENNIS. MATCH PLAY AND THE SPIN OF THE BALL. Each illustrated. 5s. net.

TILESTON (Mary W.).
DAILY STRENGTH FOR DAILY NEEDS. *Thirty-second Edition.* 3s. 6d. net. Also, India Paper, Leather, 6s. net.

UNDERHILL (Evelyn).
MYSTICISM. *Eleventh Edition.* 15s. net. THE LIFE OF THE SPIRIT AND THE LIFE OF TO-DAY. *Sixth Edition.* 7s. 6d. net. CONCERNING THE INNER LIFE. *Fifth Edition.* 2s. net. MAN AND THE SUPERNATURAL. 7s. 6d. net.

VARDON (Harry).
HOW TO PLAY GOLF. Illustrated. *Nineteenth Edition.* 5s. net. THE COMPLETE GOLFER. Illustrated. *Twenty-first Edition.* 12s. 6d. net.

WARD (A. C.).
TWENTIETH CENTURY LITERATURE: THE AGE OF INTERROGATION. 5s. net.

WATERHOUSE (Elizabeth).
A LITTLE BOOK OF LIFE AND DEATH. *Twenty-third Edition.* 2s. 6d. net.

WILDE (Oscar).
THE WORKS OF OSCAR WILDE. Seventeen Volumes. Each 6s. 6d. net. Some also Fcap. 8vo, 2s. 6d. net. 1, LORD ARTHUR SAVILE'S CRIME AND THE PORTRAIT OF MR. W. H. 2, THE DUCHESS OF PADUA. 3, POEMS. 4, LADY WINDERMERE'S FAN. 5, A WOMAN OF NO IMPORTANCE. 6, AN IDEAL HUSBAND. 7, THE IMPORTANCE OF BEING EARNEST. 8, A HOUSE OF POMEGRANATES. 9, INTENTIONS. 10, DE PROFUNDIS AND PRISON LETTERS. 11, ESSAYS. 12, SALOME, A FLORENTINE TRAGEDY, AND LA SAINTE COURTISANE. 13, A CRITIC IN PALL MALL. 14, SELECTED PROSE OF OSCAR WILDE. 15, ART AND DECORATION. 16, FOR LOVE OF THE KING: A Burmese Masque (5s. net). 17, VERA, OR THE NIHILISTS.

WOLFE (Humbert).
THE UNKNOWN GODDESS. *Second Edition.* 5s. net.

A SELECTION OF SERIES
THE ANTIQUARY'S BOOKS
Each, illustrated, Demy 8vo, 10s. 6d. net. A series of volumes dealing with various branches of English Antiquities.

THE ARDEN SHAKESPEARE
Demy 8vo, 6s. net each volume

An edition of Shakespeare in Single Plays. Edited with a full Introduction, Textual Notes, and a Commentary at the foot of the page. The edition is now complete in thirty-nine volumes.

CLASSICS OF ART
Edited by Dr. J. H. W. LAING

Illustrated. Wide Royal 8vo, from 15s. net to £3 3s. net. A Library of Art dealing with Great Artists and with branches of Art.

THE "COMPLETE" SERIES
Illustrated. Demy 8vo, from 5s. net to 18s. net. A series of books on the chief Sports and Pastimes, comprehensive, lucid and authoritative.

EIGHT BOOKS BY R. S. SURTEES
With the Original Illustrations in Colour by J. LEECH and others.

Fcap. 8vo, 6s. net and 7s. 6d. net

ASK MAMMA; HANDLEY CROSS; HAWBUCK GRANGE; HILLINGDON HALL; JORROCKS'S JAUNTS AND JOLLITIES; MR. SPONGE'S SPORTING TOUR; MR. FACEY ROMFORD'S HOUNDS; PLAIN OR RINGLETS?

THE FAITHS: VARIETIES OF CHRISTIAN EXPRESSION
Edited by L. P. JACKS, M.A., D.D., LL.D.

Crown 8vo, 5s. net each volume

The first volumes are: THE ANGLO-CATHOLIC FAITH; MODERNISM IN THE ENGLISH CHURCH; THE FAITH AND PRACTICE OF THE QUAKERS; CONGREGATIONALISM; THE FAITH OF THE ROMAN CHURCH; THE LIFE AND FAITH OF THE BAPTISTS; THE PRESBYTERIAN CHURCHES; METHODISM; THE EVANGELICAL MOVEMENT IN THE ENGLISH CHURCH; THE UNITARIANS.

THE GATEWAY LIBRARY
Fcap. 8vo, 3s. 6d. net each volume

WORKS BY H. BELLOC, ARNOLD BENNETT, E. F. BENSON, GEORGE A. BIRMINGHAM, MARJORIE BOWEN, G. K. CHESTERTON, A. CLUTTON-BROCK, JOSEPH CONRAD, J. H. CURLE, GEORGE GISSING, GERALD GOULD, KENNETH GRAHAME, A. P. HERBERT, W. H. HUDSON, RUDYARD KIPLING, E. V. KNOX, JACK LONDON, E. V. LUCAS, ROBERT LYND, ROSE MACAULAY, JOHN MASEFIELD, A. A. MILNE, C. E. MONTAGUE, ARTHUR MORRISON, EDEN PHILLPOTTS, MARMADUKE PICKTHALL, CHARLES G. D. ROBERTS, R. L. STEVENSON and OSCAR WILDE.

THE LITTLE GUIDES
Illustrated and with Maps. 65 Volumes. Small Pott 8vo, 4s. net to 7s. 6d. net.

POCKETABLE GUIDES TO THE COUNTIES OF ENGLAND AND WALES AND TO WELL-KNOWN DISTRICTS AT HOME AND ABROAD.

PLAYS
Fcap. 8vo, 3s. 6d. net each

KISMET (Paper, 2s. net); MILESTONES; AN IDEAL HUSBAND; THE WARE CASE; GENERAL POST; THE GREAT ADVENTURE; THE HONEYMOON; ACROSS THE BORDER (Crown 8vo); THE SAME STAR; GOOD-MORNING, BILL! (Crown 8vo); THE UNKNOWN WARRIOR (Crown 8vo, 7s. 6d. net).

METHUEN'S HALF-CROWN AND TWO SHILLING LIBRARIES
These are series of copyright works of general literature. They contain many books by distinguished writers.

Write for Complete Lists